Another magical book from Madeline K. Adams. *La Femme* takes us into the mysterious world of the Sacred Feminine. This book truly is food for the soul and sustenance for the spirit. It invites us to dance with our Feminine Essence, to participate fully in our soul journey, and to find our way back home to the Creatress within ourselves.

— FRANCHELLE OFSOSKÉ-WYBER SPIRITUAL TEACHER AND MENTOR

There is power conveyed in the pure release of honest thought and feeling that is incredibly gentle. I Love its authenticity.

— FAYE ALAIN AUTHOR OF *DESERT ROAD* AND *HER TRUTH*

Madeline K. Adams writes about the return of the modern-day Hestia, and the Yin Intelligence of the Feminine. A portent for us to honour, value and protect the Feminine in our current world.

— SUZANNE GLENDINNING CLINICAL PSYCHOLOGIST

A new voice re-defining Feminine Essence for the creation of a new Aquarian Era.

— MURRAY BEAUCHAMP AUTHOR OF *THE CRYPTIC CYCLE* AND SOON TO BE PUBLISHED - *MESSAGES FOR GAIA*

Madeline K. Adams has written her book right at the exact time that the Sacred Feminine is unfolding as the next step of human evolution.

She brings alive the ancient goddesses to our modern times and shows simple and efficient ways to use their archetypal energy for yourself.

This book is written in a universal context. Madeline exposes many ways to go beyond the boundaries of your stories, of your personality to explore the jewels of sacred space. Not only is there abundant wisdom in this book but you can also see it as a practical and enriching guide to embrace the Sacred Feminine in your daily life.

— Monique Leurink Developer of Diamond Astrology - A New Dimension in the World of the Stars

LA FEMME GODDESS OF THE SACRED FLAME

LA FEMME GODDESS OF THE SACRED FLAME

COLOUR THE WORLD WITH THE BEAUTY OF YOUR SOUL

MADELINE K. ADAMS

Copyright © 2022 by Madeline K. Adams

All rights reserved.

No part of this book may be reproduced in any form or by any electronic or mechanical means, including information storage and retrieval systems, without written permission from the publisher, except for the use of brief quotations in a book review.

This book is not intended as a substitute for the professional medical advice. Any use of information in this book is at the reader's discretion and risk. The author intends only to offer information of a general nature. Neither the author nor the publisher can be held responsible for any loss, claim or damage arising out of the use or misuse of suggestions made, the failure to take medical advice, or for any material on third party websites.

First Published: 22 February 2022

A catalogue record of this book is held at the National Library of New Zealand

ISBN# 978-0-473-60651-0 Amazon
ISBN# 978-0-473-60653-4 Kindle
ISBN# 978-0-473-60750-0 Ingram

Roslyn Publishing
P O Box 32276
Auckland 0744
New Zealand

You are Magic,

You are Sacred

You are Soul

Sacredness

*At the heart of everyone
there is a sacred space
a secret place where
hides your inner gold*

*An inner glow, a passion
Illuminates the darkness
With energy that dances to
The music of your song*

*Hestia's eternal flame is
Calling you home, to feel her
Essence of Stillness and Light*

~ **Hestia**

CONTENTS

Preface — xv
Introduction — xix

PART I
THE CREATRESS JOURNEY

1. The Creatress Way — 3
2. Maker of Magic — 9
3. Becoming — 13
4. Soul Presence — 19

PART II
HESTIA'S SACRED FLAME

5. Hestia's Story — 27
6. The Hestia Wound — 33
7. Hestia's Return — 37
8. Sacred Space — 41

PART III
FEMININE WAYS OF KNOWING

An Awakened Creatress — 49
9. Feminine Ways of Knowing — 51
10. Body Wisdom — 53
11. Heart Intelligence — 57
12. Intuition — 61
13. Imagination — 65
14. Psychic Knowing — 69
15. Feminine Presence — 71

PART IV
THE YIN INTELLIGENCE OF HEART

A Love Token	77
16. The Wounded Heart	79
17. Healing The Heart	81
18. Heart Wisdom	87

PART V
THE GREAT MYSTERY

Womb Magic	97
19. Form and Formlessness	99
20. Chaos & Creativity	101
21. Darkness and Light	105
22. Womb Magic	109

PART VI
ANCIENT FEMININE ARCHETYPES

Persephone's Dance	113
23. Ancient Goddesses	115
24. Stories We Tell Ourselves	119
25. Permission, Crossroads and Choices	123

PART VII
NEW STORIES ~ NEW ARCHETYPES

Child of the Universe	131
26. New Archetypes	133
27. New Stories ~ New Realities	143
28. Magic of the Inner Child	149

PART VIII
WISDOM FOR A NEW WORLD

On Angel's Wings	157
29. Sacred Beauty of Soul	159
30. World of a Creatress	163
FEMME ~ Le parfum ~ Feminine Essence	173
Feminine Essence	175
One Last Thing …..	176

Poems	177
Acknowledgments	179
About the Author	181
Also by Madeline K. Adams	183
Sources from Other Writers	185
Connection	187
La Femme Speaks ~ Quotes	189
Notes	195

PREFACE

Once upon a time, there was a long forgotten Age when the Feminine powers of creativity, co-operation and sacredness were woven into the tapestry of our everyday lives.

La Femme spoke to me in the still of the night at a time when the veils of consciousness grows thin, whispering her words of wisdom from long ago. Her words arose out of the Aether in sentences that carried a ring of truth to them, resonating with a clarity and simplicity that awakened feelings of aliveness within my heart.

The writing of *La Femme* began to morph over time as she expressed more of her truth to me, reminding me of something lost, an ancient Creatress way of living. This was becoming a story about the dynamic mystery and sacredness of Feminine Essence within us all.

My working title for this book began as *The Art of Creatress Magic* and just as I thought the book was finished, I awoke one morning with the knowing that I must write about Hestia, the Forgotten Goddess. Her story centres around a sacred flame and this flame grew to symbolise the sacredness of the pure Essence of the Feminine.

I began to give myself the time and space needed to honour the sacredness of my Feminine Essence. I focused on empowerment (power that comes from within), and I stepped into my power as a Creatress living my truth and loving my authentic self, and I came to understand that:

My Feminine Essence is My Soul Power

I remembered a classic movie with Robert De Niro called *the Scent of a Woman*. There is a sensual scene where he plays a blind man who dances with a beautiful woman. He attunes to her presence, sensing her by the beauty of her essence. This then reminded me of the perfume I loved to wear as a young woman called *Femme*.

Marcel Rochas created this perfume for his wife Hélène as an ode to Femininity and to Love, and a heart felt tribute to her Feminine Essence.

> "This spicy fruity Chypre .. a velvety plum tone awakens an intense sensuality with its base notes of sandalwood, patchouli and vetiver arousing mysterious feelings, stirred even further by rose absolute, ylang and jasmine.
> A deeply sensual opulence complimented with the crispness of lemon, neroli and bergamot's Gourmand citrus notes ... warmed by spicy hints of cumin, cinnamon and cloves."
>
> ~ Olfactory description of **Femme** du parfum by Rochas

A new philosophy had begun to emerge out of the writing of my memoir *The Odyssey of a Creatress*. My story of soul awakening that came out of my journey as a seeker of my soul's truth after years of feeling lost and invisible.

I felt called to question the beliefs and values
I had taken for granted in my life until this moment
My instincts began to tell me there is another way

This other way has led me on an inner journey
To hear the subtle language of my soul and to
Uncover the core essence of my feminine self

My second book *The Sacred Dance of Soul* flowed from the first as I began to explore the personal meaning of soul in my life. I stepped into the unfolding dance of a Creatress and took the journey into my heart to know myself as Soul.

Now the story of La Femme ~ the pure Essence of the Feminine has found its way into the pages of this book.

I am in my 70's, and for years I have been waking to words that arise spontaneously into my consciousness, often laden with archetypal symbolism that has a way of capturing simple truths and universal wisdom.

I have found myself writing about the Goddess Hestia and her sacred healing powers. Her sacred flame illuminates my senses and my inner passion calls me to live in alignment with my sacred Feminine Essence.

My life as a Creatress has become a journey of discovery. I now know that Creatress Magic arises out of a well of feminine intelligence deep within me and her presence has become the pathway to finding my joy.

> As I type Creatress into my computer
> 'Word' decides to auto-correct to Creatures.
> No, I don't mean creatures I mean **CREATRESS**

The word *CREATRESS* conjures a vision of strength, and the empowerment of the pure creative essence of the Feminine. To know the Creatress requires us to expand our definition of words such as **strength** and **power** and begin to recognise their feminine expression, and to value the creative forces that are essentially invisible and magnetic mystery.

I began to see that we are in need of new names for new ways of being and the Creatress became the first of these to make her presence known to me as I listened into the whisperings of my soul.

INTRODUCTION

La Femme ~

***A philosophy of the pure essence
of Woman, her truth, her beauty,
her passion and her power contained
within the Sacredness of her Soul.***

La Femme unashamedly explores the Sacred Feminine within each of us, leading us into our hidden depths where we commune with our Feminine Essence; uncovering a creative force that by its very nature is a sacred and magical mystery.

We may fear our feminine essence and think of it as a weakness, or we may merely project our inner feminine onto others in our outer world; we may simply be too shy to show this sacred part of ourselves for fear of appearing to be vulnerable, too sensitive, or leaving ourselves open to abuse or ridicule by others.

We seem to have forgotten that we are as much feminine as we are masculine as the Chinese describes so elegantly with the simplicity of their Yin/Yang symbol. We wonder why we feel that something is missing, some element that would bring balance and harmony into our lives.

After many years of strengthening my connection to my Inner World, I now know in my bones that my Feminine Essence illuminates a Creatress way of *Soul~full living:* ~

> *Creative Intelligence of Feminine Essence*
> *is your Soul Power*

La Femme provides the Feminine perspective needed to reclaim our lost gifts, and she offers us the ability to bring balance, peace and harmony into our everyday lives.

The myth of Hestia re-kindles the ancient archetype of a forgotten Goddess who attends her Sacred Flame.

Hestia calls us to create a sacred space to relax into as we attune to our inner world in a focused way. She invites us to become real to ourselves, meaning loving yourself just as you are and giving yourself permission to become authentically you, as you rekindle your memory of the Goddess of the Sacred Flame.

There are young women today who are finding their voice and growing their courage to speak their truth. Their words and actions are making a difference in the world and their empowered Feminine presence is playing a formidable catalytic part in the creation of a new world.

A new philosophy is emerging into consciousness, calling you to live guided by your Feminine intelligence.

I invite you to own the power of your *Femme Essence* that resonates as authenticity within your heart, embrace the unfolding grace of your *Creatress Magic* and experience the joy of living in atunement with your Soul.

Goethe's quote captures this potentiality beautifully:

> ***"Whatever you can do or***
> ***dream you can, begin it.***
> ***Boldness has genius,***
> ***power and magic in it."***

Trust in the outer world grows as you learn to live guided by your inner wise self and you discover the immense power that is the *Magic of pure Essence*.

To discover a new philosophy of how to live
as an empowered Creatress honouring
Hestia's sacred flame and
your Femme Essence

Begin the journey.....

PART I
THE CREATRESS JOURNEY

A Creatress Takes The Inner Path …..

CHAPTER 1
THE CREATRESS WAY

*A Creatress knows herself to be a
deeply feminine woman who is ready to
take off the mask that has kept her hidden
She embodies her feminine intelligence
And steps into her creative power*

*T*he Sacred Feminine within each of us is a creative force which by its very nature is magical mystery. She opens herself to a world of Cosmic consciousness, she listens into the wisdom in her heart and she leads us into our hidden depths where we commune with the sacredness of our soul.

The Creatress Way presents us with a new way of living that requires us to value the invisible mystery realms of intelligence that surrounds us in every moment. We are energy that by its very nature is constantly in motion, ever changing, flowing and renewing itself. Our challenge is to awaken to an expanded and more inclusive consciousness of self that honours all dimensions of our human experience, including the subtle, magical and invisible presence of our soul intelligence.

Although you may think of yourself on a spiritual journey, your individual task is to become an embodied soul and to express the unique beauty and truth that lives within you. When we honour this presence we awaken to a power that is immense and amazing.

Our inner feminine knowing comes from the creative expression of our heart's intelligence ~ this is the task of becoming a Creatress.

> *To be able to value our heart's intelligence requires that we redefine the meaning of words such as Courage, Strength, Power, Intelligence and Creativity from a feminine perspective*

If you find your self feeling invisible or have lost your way, secretly believing that you have failed in some way, then maybe it is time for you to overcome your anxiety, doubts and fear and to begin to trust in the power of your heart's intelligence and your innate knowing alive within every cell of your being.

The path of a Creatress is a different way of living. She does not look outside of herself for guidance, rather she trusts herself and moves through her life deeply connected to her heart's wisdom that resonates with her personal truth. You have to become courageous to embrace your feminine essence in this way.

Become the Artist

When you choose this path that resonates with your truth, this changes your perceptions of who you are in the depths of your being. You find yourself able to own your unique gifts, and step more fully into the authentic expression of your soul. This leads you into a state of happiness and fulfilment.

> *Walking the path of an empowered woman,*
> *you claim your inner authority and live from*
> *a place of authenticity that expresses*
> *the pure essence of your true beauty.*

You have the soul of an artist and as you learn to trust your inner guidance this brings powerful changes into your life in ways beyond belief.

As you become receptive to your Feminine Ways of knowing, this creates an intimate relationship with your Body that is home to the physical presence of your Soul.

The first step to awakening to this inner power is to consciously create a sacred space in which to commune with your Feminine Intelligence. Her energy is a mysterious magnetic force which can only begin to be known through life's experiences.

∼

You are taking on the mantle of a Creatress who knows how to connect to her creative power when you feel into the depths of your inner knowing, trust your intuition and learn to follow the calling of your soul.

Life becomes an unfolding creative process with many twists and turns and surprises along the way. You become a maker of magic and you blossom into the rhythms of your soul when you are willing to follow subtle guidance as it comes to you.

When you learn how to live this way, you find yourself able to let go of old programming and the fear based need to always be in control. The Feminine has no need for control, structured plans or scientific analysis. These are the domain of the Masculine way we have all spent many years learning to master.

You will discover your innate intelligence is a force freely available to you. You only need to let go of old limiting beliefs and trust in your inner knowing, follow its guidance and be willing to step into a new story. One that reflects the truth and beauty of your authentic self.

Your soul speaks to you all of the time in powerful ways that are far beyond your understanding.

Nature, the Earth and all living beings trust in this Cosmic Intelligence that is the aliveness of the Sacred Dance that moves in rhythm to the sounds of the Universe.

Let's take a look at the ways in which a Creatress moves through the day that are so different to the rules and structures that have inculcated our thinking and defined our accepted ways of being, thereby limiting our ability to own the amazingly powerful and creative presence of our Feminine Essence.

CHAPTER 2
MAKER OF MAGIC

A Creatress is a maker of magic
Her heart is open, she feels into her soul
To know that which is true for her

Magic is akin to good design ~ simplicity and imagination in action, it is the stuff of dreams come true. Art and Magic are related to each other, for the creation of art is a magical process. Art delights us with its magic and surprises us with its power.

A Creatress has the soul of an artist with access to the inner knowledge of her dark feminine. She is Cosmic energy and she vibrates with the intelligence of her inner world which is a rich resource of guidance showing her the way to live. She knows that her physical manifestation is only one part of her wholeness and that her Feminine Intelligence and her Heart Wisdom speak with the authentic voice of the Soul Star essence of her inner child ~ her personal expression from Source.

Magic happens all the time for some people and hardly ever for others. Becoming Real has the honesty and authenticity required to make magic possible.

Recipes for Magic have be written down in books (witches call them spells) but it is the quality of the presence of the maker of magic that makes all the difference. Magic is made up of intention and presence; and then trust, spontaneity and synchronicities facilitate the process.

I remember when I was a young child walking down the most exclusive street in my city and peering into the beautiful houses and in my innocence wondering ~ What do the people living in these houses believe about themselves and how do they use their imagination in ways that make it possible for them to have their dreams come true?

When you relax into your soul self, connect into the warmth in your heart and live from this inner place of knowing, you will notice synchronicities and magic abound. This happens when we fall in love. All of our past just fades away and we believe for a moment that love is possible as we feel into our awakened heart.

To have time and a safe space to relax, to dream and allow the child within to play. To be able to imagine and then hold the belief that something is possible, this creates the environment for magic to happen.

Your heart is the clearest voice that speaks from your soul, and your whole body is the barometer of your soul's presence or lack thereof. Your soul calls you to be real and true and to live your life with an open and loving heart. Courage comes from having a loving heart no matter what life throws at you.

Children find it so easy to believe in magic and they are so receptive to the awe and wonder of this amazing universe we find ourselves living in. It is so important to be willing to heal our hearts, to awaken our inner child and to give ourselves the chance to believe again in magic.

Depression has become a disease of our modern age and a sign that there is a loss of connection to our soul's wisdom and the disillusionment and loss of the open hearted wonder of our unacknowledged inner child.

It requires a major paradigm shift away from all of our past memories of pain and loss and all our fears and mistrust in life, to heal the wounds within our hearts and be willing to begin again. Your soul's truth is alive within the beauty of your loving heart.

Honour the mystery, experience the magic
Ground your physical presence in time and space
And live bathed in the magnetic forces of Love

CHAPTER 3
BECOMING

We are a mystery unfolding in
The dimensions of space and time
With the task to become a unique soul
As expression of Source here on Earth
To listen to our Heart and to know at last
How to embrace Becoming as the Art of Magic

*B*eing present in the moment with trust in your inner knowing and connection to Source. Practical and magical mysteries combine and you become more than you ever imagined as you step out into your world.

Our mind tries to understand that which is beyond mind. It is the heart that enables us to feel into the truth within us. Becoming is the result of many small choices taken as we learn to follow the instinctual knowing that exists within us, and we find our self confidence grows stronger.

The Creatress Journey

A Creatress pursues a sacred calling to trust her instincts, value her intuition and be guided by the subtle messages from her Soul.

She begins by dreaming, pondering and imagining her visions of possibility. Then she asks for guidance with a clarity of intent that aligns with the longings of her heart. She takes a risk and trusts as the unfolding path reveals itself, sometimes in unexpected and mysterious ways, with a willingness to take just one small step at a time without knowing where her journey will lead. She brings new creations into form as an expression of her Soul.

Live in the Flow

She has felt the calling of her soul and she has learned how to live in the flow, and become a Creatress and Modern Mystic.

Sometimes life is about being receptive, slowing down and creating space to relax and reflect, and sometimes it is about risking and taking action or learning something new. Each has its own value and its own gifts that enrich our lives. Too much emphasis on just one of these creates an imbalance in our soul.

Follow the Energy

When you connect to your passion, you awaken to the calling of your soul and you are taken up by a current that pulls you along; only time will allow you to see where this journey leads you.

Ask yourself ~
*Was I ever taught to trust in myself
or was I encouraged to trust in the lead
of others more powerful than myself?*

When you follow where your energy draws you this allows the adventure of a creative process to unfold.

Stepping Stones

Life becomes a dance and the movements lead us along a series of stepping stones. Sometimes asking us to wait with patience until the time is right and other times asking us to step out in a new direction as an unknown path unveils itself before us.

Heart Intelligence

When we begin to walk the path of the Creatress we begin a journey that leads us into an intimate connection with our heart's wisdom. Heart energy is an intelligence that reaches far beyond the mind for it speaks from every cell of our being in the languages of Soul.

The power to create comes from an innate knowing which is an aspect of feminine intelligence that we often take for granted. We rarely take the time to place value on this powerful ability within us.

When you have developed a mature and loving relationship with your self, only then will you know how to take the heroines journey into the depths of your inner world.

The inner journey leads you to connect to your feminine intelligence calling you to heal any wounds alive in your heart so you can trust yourself enough to uncover the knowing wisdom of your soul.

When we restore our ability to truly love ourselves then we can share our love in the world. This is much needed for healing to happen on a soul level of consciousness.

The Sacred Dance

I have found that life unfolds in mysterious ways when I allow my self to be guided by the heart wisdom of my soul. I have been led into experiences I would never have chosen with my thinking/planning logos/mind. It has often been these adventures that have shown me the way to live from my pure essence, aligning me with my true path and bring experiences that surprise me and awaken me to emotions of joy and true happiness beyond my imaginings.

Creativity & the Creatress

Creatress is the archetype of the Creative Feminine. She is the eternal aliveness within each of us, and she expresses the essence of her Soul.

*She is cosmically connected to Universal Intelligence
and lightly touches the knowing realms of Source Creation*

She has learned to be still and listen into the wisdom of her heart and the innate intelligence of her body. She has developed an intimate relationship with her soul.

A Creatress is connected to nature and all who live upon the earth and she is also connected to the universal intelligence of the Cosmos. She knows that the Earth is the ground of her being which supports and nourishes her. For this reason alone she honours her body, for it is a sacred temple of her soul.

Enter into your own safe space where you are free to commune with your Essence; knowing you can be soft and gentle or when needs be strong and passionate like a lioness fiercely protecting her cubs.

Creativity takes its own time and needs a sacred space in which to transmute energy ~ the alchemy of nature transforming and manifesting into new forms

This is the Aliveness of your Becoming

CHAPTER 4
SOUL PRESENCE

*Our soul speaks to us through the intelligence
of our heart with vibrations of love that resonate
within every cell of our body as a natural
expression of our authentic self*

Our Soul is always there and yet many of us have learned not to pay heed to its presence in our lives. This distortion began long ago and yet there is a shift afoot and a new question is being posed:

What brings me joy and gives meaning to my life?

Subtle perceptions speak to us in ways that go beyond our rational thinking mind. They speak of our personal truth through the whole of our being. Our task is to awaken our sensitivity to these subtle messages:

> *Emotions* arise unbidden from some place deep within, they are messages that come from the intelligence of the heart.

Dreams take us into the unconscious realms

Visions enter our field of consciousness often with vivid colours that carry an energy charge. They awaken us to hidden emotions that have been stored within our memory body often unfelt and unacknowledged.

Psyche ~ Soul can be seen as an inner light and an aura of that surrounds us. It encompasses the gestalt of our dynamic energy blueprint that is the pure energy expression of our wholeness.

The Presence of Spirit

The focus of this book is on the inner journey to know yourself as soul. There is another realm of experience that comes from the world of spirit. We can choose to develop our perceptiveness and the ability to acknowledge it's presence. This energy that exists as spirit, I have found to be very real and present in my life at times when I have needed protection and guidance in the outer world.

Here are some of the ways in which I have experienced the visitation of spirits, each in their chosen ways.

Experiences of tastes and smells, and sometimes of a felt presence or a light body that shows up when spirit is around me.

> I remember seeing a bright light in the corner of the room soon after my mother died.

> I felt someone's hand gently brushing my brow

when no one was there.

I smelt the presence of my father as the woody scent of the factories where he had been the manager.

I recall the experience of a felt knowing that a spirit guide was present, standing close beside me when I travelled the world alone.

I could taste strawberries when the spirit of my husband's lover was present in the room.

To be conscious of these subtle energies requires trusting your experience in each moment with an openness and resonance to the natural movement and flow of energy, together with an understanding that spirit is as real as you and me.

Soul

Soul is always present within you. Soul is not just a light body, it is the pure essence of your authentic self at the core of your being.

When you learn to open your heart and listen inwardly and place your attention onto the subtle guidance that is unique to you, only then can you know the energy force of your awakened soul and feel its warmth as it emanates from within. Let yourself venture into the depths of your inner being to meet with your soul.

When you place your attention on your inner sacred flame, it becomes a glowing energy, a golden essence and a magnetic force that can be felt as a warmth in your heart and a glow in your aura, as the truth of your core essence, and the energy of your eternal soul.

Once awakened it cannot be taken from you. It is a magnetic force and the creative magic of love. When we truly love ourself, then we become real ~ a unique authentic soul.

Remember that Source is within you, it speaks to you in the voice of your inner child ~ your Soul Star self; that eternal part of you that is the magnetic power of your Sacred Soul.

The Sacred Feminine within each of us is a creative force which by its very nature is magical mystery. She leads us into our hidden depths where we commune with the sacred part of self that is our soul. She creates spaces in-between where there is room for something new to emerge, for it is in these spaces that magic happens.

I was first introduced to Sacred Space when I learned about the Greek Goddess Hestia (or Vesta as she was known in Roman times.) Her task was to keep the sacred flame alive at the centre of the city and her presence was honoured as the flame in the round hearth found at the centre of every home.

Sacredness is the experience of being touched within by the presence of Soul. Sacredness exists within us as our personal felt sense of soul and everything that exists in our known world carries this energy of sacredness.

Sacred can be found in nature and in every living thing, and in the numinous moments when we are touched by the Love that exists in and all around us.

Energy of La Femme

Those of us who dare to believe that there is more than our eyes can perceive in our 3D world. Magic happens and guidance is there for us if we can only begin to believe in the invisible, mystical and magical realms.

Habits, rituals and old ways of living prevent us from going within for new answers. We live on auto pilot, unconscious to the reality that our habits are dramatically effecting the way we live our lives.

Become empowered by the goddess Hestia as you step into your life as an artist, mystic and Creatress, knowing you are a Sacred Soul.

- I suggest you take some time out to consider new habits. Ones that honour the sacredness of yourself as Soul on this journey of becoming.
- Time spent in self reflective listening creates a space for new awareness to arise into consciousness.
- Begin by posing a question, and take time to ponder and let your imagination play with thoughts as they arise.
- Stay in a state of open waiting and willingness to perceive subtle whispers as they arise.
- Take time to slow your breathing, and come into a calm, spacious and open state of being.

- Being with yourself in this way allows you to remember this calm aliveness and peace within.
- Take this way of being with you as you step out into your everyday living.
- Create a sacred ritual for yourself to connect to the sacred flame within and feel this focused energy within you.
- Allowing yourself the time and space to go within and connect to the sacredness of your soul and live from this place of beauty and grace unfolding.

As we take on the presence of these subtle energy fields as valid and true and we become conscious of the ways in which our every thought and deed effects the quality of presence we shine into our world.

We have a Presence,
who we are at the core of our being
that others can sense without the need for words
We perceive this subtle energy in others too

Today I awoke thinking of writing about the Greek Goddess Hestia, the temple priestess, keeper of the Sacred Flame.

Let's explore the myth of Hestia to honour the sacredness of our lives, a quality greatly needed in todays dystopian world where great suffering and injustices abound.

PART II
HESTIA'S SACRED FLAME

The Forgotten Goddess of Sacred Spaces …..

CHAPTER 5

HESTIA'S STORY

Hestia honours the sacredness of all living creatures
She honours the sacredness of the Earth
and the sacredness of Soul

Hestia is present at the round Hearth (which contains the words heart and earth) where the warmth of a sacred flame becomes the focus of her quiet domain. In today's world she is a Wisdom Keeper of Sacredness. She honours the sacredness within everything, your home, your heart and your world.

Ancient symbols for the Goddess Hestia are:

A ***sacred living flame*** contained
within the **circle** of a **round hearth**

Hestia the Goddess of the Sacred Flame represents your inner focused passion. Through her you connect to the sacredness within you ~ your inner sanctuary. The secret space wherein you are virgin ~ meaning whole unto yourself. Your sacred centre from which shines her dancing flame which emanates as your golden glow.

Many Goddesses have been written about in my earlier books. It's now time for the myth of the forgotten Goddess Hestia to shine her light and so I tell her story ~

Hestia's Story

The original version from Ancient Greece …..

> Hestia was the first born child of the Titans Cronus and Rhea whose children became the original twelve Gods and Goddesses of Olympia. Hestia's father Cronus feared a prophesy that a child of his would usurp his power and so the myth goes, he swallowed each of his children. Hestia became the first of the children to be swallowed by her father.
> Eventually, Rhea found a way of saving her newborn baby Zeus by offering Cronus a stone wrapped in swaddling clothes to swallow instead which he did. He then regurgitated all of the children he had previously swallowed and so they miraculously all tumbled out alive and well.
>
> Hestia was the first to be swallowed and the last to be set free and so she was the child who spent the most time in the dark inner-world within her father and some of that time she was completely alone. This experience of powerlessness taught her how to surrender her need for the egos desires

for overt power over others and endowed her with the ability to be able to focus within. She became a Goddess who had no desire to be part of the Olympians quests for fame or their joisting for political power.

She did not accept the marriage proposals from both Apollo and Poseidon, instead she freely chose to remain virginal (meaning whole unto herself ~ belonging to no man.) She decided instead to claim her personal power by making wise choices for herself that were in alignment with her Soul.

Hestia willingly agreed to leave Olympia, to make a place for Dionysus to become one of the twelve Gods of the Pantheon.
Hestia was given a status above all others as keeper of this Sacred Flame. This flame was thought to represent the sacred centre of the city and so it was important that it was kept alive as a symbol of protection and abundance and the source of inspiration and renewal of the life giving aspects of the Goddess. She was endowed with the privileged of having the freedom of the city.
Unlike the other Gods and Goddesses who were worshiped with statues and had temples built in their honour, she was honoured by the fire at the heart of the city and worshiped by the fire alight in the hearth at the centre of every home.

Hestia Became the Goddess of the People

Hestia became a sacred Priestess who touched peoples lives in a very personal way. Her presence created an experience of stillness, serenity and the sacredness of sanctuary.

She held a place of privilege and she was given powers and authority within the city and was valued by all. She was given the best of offerings and became the Goddess of the Sacred Flame of Feminine Essence.

She was the keeper of important documents, she was given the right to own property and she held the power to grant freedom to repentant prisoners.

She was the Goddess of Architecture with the focus on creation of a home with a hearth as the central focus, to contain her sacred flame. This also applied to the building of a city around a central space where people could gather together, a place where the Flame of the city burned; a place of community and hospitality and most of all a sacred place of sanctuary and protection.

She chose her vow of sacred sanctuary, she honoured the sacred flame and she was free to embrace her emotional sensuality and the creative pleasure and sacredness of her sexuality.

Hestia chose to live a simple life, she did not need the adornments of Aphrodite, nor did she desire the role of wife. She refused the offer of marriage by the Gods Apollo and Poseidon. Rather she choose to remain Virgin in the sense of being whole unto herself which meant that she then belonged to no man.

She held the power to initiate others into the healing experience of sacred union, a connection between two souls. This became part of the ancient sexual rites carried out in honour of the fertilising power of the Goddess. Any children born from these sexual encounters were considered divine and welcomed as children of the royal court some of whom took on a special destiny of the royal succession.

Hestia created a sense of sanctuary where people could come to experience sacred space and to be present to themselves in a way that nurtured and healed their soul. She freely chose a life of quiet simplicity as sacred priestess and keeper of the sacred flame.

This did not mean that she lived a life of celibacy, rather her sexuality became a healing experience for those who communed with her presence. They arrived needing sanctuary and left greatly changed by the experience of their encounter with her. Her sacredness extended to her sensuality and sexuality became a sacred act. This was at a time when sexuality, sensuality and sacredness where considered as one. She made sacred the three alchemical creation moments of conception, birth and death as moments in which we honour the sacredness of Soul.

Hestia was present in every home as the flame alive at the round hearth in the centre of every dwelling, there being no temples built in her honour. She preferred a simple life of quiet contemplation. She has become the forgotten goddess and her flame has dimmed, and many have forgotten the soul's need to honour sacred space in their lives.

Hestia reminds us of the connection between our Heart and our Soul that come together through the physicality of being fully present in our body. She honours the sacred in simple everyday rituals of our lives and she knows the passion that is the sacred flame within our Soul. Her sacredness extended to her sensuality, and for her sexuality was a sacred act. She had a natural beauty and gracefulness, a joyful creative passion, and a gentle peacefulness. Her passion emanates as the bright light of her soul's inner glow.

When we honour Hestia in our lives we are valuing the physicality of our body, the creativity of our passion and the desires of our hearts as we find our way home to the eternal aliveness that is the Feminine Essence of our Soul.

CHAPTER 6
THE HESTIA WOUND

*H*estia's story changes as we move into the later Roman version where she is re-named Vesta and her role in the community becomes that of a Vestal Virgin and she becomes controlled by male dominated rules and bound by an oath of celibacy on pain of death.

The emergence of this distorted Roman derivation of the original Greek story became the myth of Vesta. There was a denial of the sacredness of her creative essence, and a loss of her freedom to express her inner passion, including her right to freely follow the path of her own choosing. Gone are her healing powers of sacred sexual union, and her light begins to diminish. These changes to Hestia's rights and ways of living initiate the wounding of the Feminine denying the true essence of Hestia and her Sacred Flame.

The Priestess Vesta's story:

> Lost in translation from Greek Goddess Hestia to Roman Priestess Vesta. Hestia's honoured place amongst the Gods became dramatically altered by the time the Romans began to acknowledge her presence. They called her Vesta, the keeper of the sacred flame but they reduced her role down to being a vestal virgin and she was made to deny her sacred sexual powers. Her punishment for disobeying her vow of chastity was the humiliation of being publicly whipped then bound and carried into an underground crypt where she would be walled up with only a candle and a little food and left to die a torturously slow and painful death. Thus the split between the Goddess Hestia with the creative healing powers of her sacred sexuality began. Her virginal feminine essence (the true meaning of *virgin*) previously honoured by the Greeks was reduced to the role of Vesta as the sexually celibate priestesses of Rome and daughters of the Patriarchy.

The rise of Patriarchy

Enter the Roman kings and their relationship of domination over Hestia's presence and their responses fearing the threat she held towards their rights of succession to the throne of Rome.

Before this time the kings of Rome were chosen from the sons of Hestia virgin goddesses. The most famous of these was Romulus the first King of Rome. This was a time when Hestia was venerated and her sexuality was considered to be the sacred and fertilising power of the Goddess.

By the 5th Century the Emperor Theodosius finally abolished the worship of Hestia to prevent her offspring becoming claimants to the throne.

Hestia went underground and continued to be active for a while and over time her flame became diminished. In this way the rituals that honoured a sense of sacredness in everyday life became lost to us. This loss of an inner experience of sacred sanctuary and the quiet and peaceful space it brought to every home began to be forgotten.

This loss of her presence in our lives is the story of the wounding of the Feminine that occurred with the denial of our sexual fire grounded in the sacredness within our bodies. We began to view the Feminine as a split between virgin/whore. Sexuality was no longer a sacred pleasure, with evil now projected onto this natural part of our being fully alive.

Hestia as Vesta lost her autonomy and instead became a possession of the Patriarchy (distorted masculine) to be used as he sought fit. No longer was sexuality sacred, it became a source of power to be used to control and dominate, and the inner creative forces of the Feminine became denigrated and disavowed throughout the world.

With this split between sexuality as a sacred act of the Goddess Hestia, and the nun like celibacy of Vesta with her sexless role as a vestal virgin as she began to completely denying the transformative and healing power of her sacred sexuality.

The Hestia wound became embedded in a culture that found evermore ways to deny and denigrate the Sacred Feminine. The overtones of this wounding of our perceptions of this innate soul power of feminine energy has reverberated throughout history. Our relationship to this primal feminine essence needs to be addressed by us all.

*The loss of Sacredness has become
the Feminine Wound*

CHAPTER 7

HESTIA'S RETURN

Hestia, no longer the Forgotten Goddess Becomes the Keeper of our Soul's Passion

*A*s we bring alive the qualities of Hestia the forgotten Goddess, we begin to heal the pain hidden deep within us. Hestia is deeply connected to her heart and the earth is the ground of her being. Her symbol is a flame within the circle of a hearth. A circle contains a promise that cannot be broken, a symbol of your hearts truth, a love token. The Hearth is where we come together to be present in our hearts and grounded to the earth.

Heart and Earth ~ Love and Presence.

She is the Sacred Flame alive within us all, and she is home to the warmth and passion of our Soul. Her Sacred Flame is a symbol of the pure essence of the eternal Self as Soul. Her flame draws us into our inner self where our

Heart and our Being come together in the promise of true relationship with our our unique and authentic soul.

The return of Hestia brings with it a love of quiet sacred space, an honouring of the creative and healing powers of the feminine, and the sacredness of sexuality. She re-ignites the flame within us that is the aliveness and passion of our source essence. Hestia does not seek the limelight but prefers quiet spaces found in nature and time and space just to be present to the world within and all around her. She brings a sense of sacredness to the everyday simplicity of her life. She recognises that simplicity has an elegance and grace to it that is restful to the soul.

This inner world of sensitivity and subtle knowing is the secret space where the precious gifts of your soul lie hidden away waiting to be brought alive. As you awaken this sacred flame within, you step into your soul power and take on the magnetic warm and glowing presence of your sacred self.

It is in this space between where magic happens. It cannot be defined, controlled, commercialised or predicted for it is the place of potentiality from which creativity arises.

When we go beyond the programming of our rational mind and enter into the spaciousness between our thoughts, only then can we uncover the wealth of intelligence that is freely available to us all. It is from this Sacred Space that Hestia creates her magic.

Hestia means Essence. She is La Femme the empowered feminine (Woman) with a strong sense of her Femininity.

She is comfortable with her own company. She is wise beyond her years and she sees the sacredness within everything and everyone. She is honest and authentically true to herself. Her inner passion feeds her soul and she lives the qualities of simplicity and sacredness expressed gracefully through the intensity of her quiet presence.

Hestia's home becomes a place of retreat and rest that carries the healing vibrations of a sanctuary. A quiet space where souls come to recuperate and heal themselves. She knows the power of solitude and has learned to connect into the innate intelligence within herself.

Hestia's flame reminds us that our Soul contains a sacred essence which can only be uncovered by venturing into the truth and beauty that is alive within us. She holds space open to be able to receive guidance from Cosmic intelligence as she listens with an open heart.

Hestia's essence is a powerful creative and magnetic force that invites us to honour our calling. The flame she tends is symbolic of this sacred passion that is so often hidden away in the recesses of our Soul.

There are many aspects to this Feminine energy alive within us. I have found that by honouring Hestia who was the first of the Goddesses, I am able to begin to heal old ways of being, let go of false beliefs and release the wounds I have carried in my heart.

Healing my wounded self, restores my sense of sacredness in my everyday life. My sacred sensuality is a welcome part of my sacredness and my passion becomes a fire of illumination that I take with me into my world.

Hestia's sacred flame awakens us to the knowledge of an inner power, a natural expression of innate wisdom that comes from the heart intelligence of our Soul.

I become virgin as I own Hestia's sacred flame

CHAPTER 8
SACRED SPACE

Finding the Sacred Space Within ~
Your Creative Essence & Your Soul Power

Sacred can be found in nature and in every living thing, and in the numinous moments when we are touched by the love and beauty that exists in and all around us. Everything that exists outside of us in our known world carries this energy of sacredness.

Our Sacredness is home to our personal felt sense of soul. There is both simplicity and complexity to be found in this space and a beauty and truth in its aliveness. Miracles go from possibilities to probability, and potentialities becoming reality.

Sacred can be felt when we gaze into the deep beauty of the night sky. This sacredness flows through us when we witness the birth of a child, a felt experience of being touched by the presence of Soul.

The Divine is suggestive of something out there, beyond our reach, up in the heavens, the divine mystery of 'All That Is.'

When we give our selves time and space to be open and become present to the 'What Is' in each moment, we create an opening to be able to sense the wonder and magic that is this pure essence of life itself.

If sacredness is within us and all around us, the way to honour this sacredness is to slow down and take a moment to feel into this aliveness. There is a beautifully simple meditation I enjoy ~ *Re-kindle my Sacred Flame.*

When we take a moment to be in a quiet reflective space, we are choosing to honour the sacredness of our existence. This is the dimension where the pure essence of Love exists. We can feel into this with our hearts, as we open to an experience of unconditional love. In these quiet in-between spaces we are able to meet our true self.

When you give time and space to honour the sacred and relax into its spaciousness, this opens a door that will lead you gracefully into the depths of your soul. It is from this Sacred Space that a Creatress makes her magic.

There are gifts hidden in this deep place which when awoken can become the source of great happiness and fulfilment. The hidden gift of your inner gold, home to the authenticity of your truth and your unique Soul Essence.

Creating Space for Yourself

Many of us long to fit in, to belong and so we dampen down our unique sparkle as a way of being accepted, conforming to the norms of the society we find ourselves living in.

Adolescence is a time when the desire to break free takes over and we search for new ways to express our individuality, to stand out, be different and create our own unique pathway as we navigate our world and find our own way of living.

Would you like to recapture some of the excitement of living in the moment with a sense of hope for the future and an unwavering belief in yourself?

Ask yourself these questions ~

> Am I an Artist?
> Could I become a Modern Mystic?
> Can I live the magical life of a Creatress?

Do you remember a time when you believed that anything was possible; when you were willing to flow from one experience to another without the need to known the outcome?

This is the way of a Creatress who lives guided by her Feminine Intelligence. She remembers that Source is within her; it is home to the eternal aliveness of her Feminine Essence. There is no time like now to recapture some of this excitement for living in the moment, with a sense of hope for the future and an unwavering belief in yourself. You can become a Creatress who lives gracefully guided by the feminine intelligence of her soul.

Create your own Sacred Space

There is a tendency to look outside of ourselves for our answers. Give yourself time to honour your inner world as an act of sacred presence and the space to be present to the reality of this physical world of form.

When you create a sacred space in your home you are paying homage to this rich place of mystery, wisdom and power that exists within you.

Sacred Space and time spent in self reflection creates the freedom to be able to make new choices, as you uncover your passion and become real and true to your soul self.

Symbols have a way of speaking directly to the Soul without the need for words. So gather together personal treasures that speak to something deep within you. Have a special space in which to place these treasured items. Make it a place of beauty that resonates within your heart and reflects your unique and personal sense of self.

I have found there are core elements of my sacred space that do not change and other elements that do as I grow into becoming more of my authentic self.

> I have a small hexagonal victorian table
> that I inherited from my grandmother
> which I painted the colour of

> violets in memory of her

> There I placed an array of symbolic items
> Chosen because they speak to my soul

> I add a flower, a tarot card, a poem
> or change the colour of my candle
> depending on the energies of the moment

Making time to be in this sacred space reminds me to breathe into the sacredness within me, and as I light my candle, this becomes a symbol to awaken my sacred flame at the centre of my being.

This visual feast of symbols & images before me reaches into my soul, awakening the oft forgotten parts of myself that sometimes become lost to me in my busy outer world.

> *I know I have a deep well of creative power within me*
> *and I am far more than the sum of my parts,*
> *I am magic and mystery combined.*
> *I give space to listen into my heart and remind myself*
> *that I am a loving Soul on a journey of Becoming.*
> *I give thanks to all that I am.*

Hestia is the Goddess of Inner focus who honours the sacredness of our everyday lives. Her presence in my life has lead me to embody my Feminine Essence and open me to my subtle Feminine ways of knowing. Hestia says ~

> *I commit to nourishing the power of my passion*
> *And the sacred aliveness of my inner flame*

PART III
FEMININE WAYS OF KNOWING

Open Your Heart and Hear the Languages of Soul …..

AN AWAKENED CREATRESS

I am an awakened Creatress with
The ability to imagine new possibilities
I have the insight of a modern mystic
And I know her love as grace unfolding

I resonate with the truth in my heart
I trust the wisdom of my innate knowing
I dance to the music of my unique soul song

My feminine intelligence aligns with my Soul
I embrace the Mystical laws of the Cosmos
I know that I am Love made manifest

CHAPTER 9

FEMININE WAYS OF KNOWING

I invite you to become receptive to your Feminine Intelligence, an immense inner power that emanates as innate wisdom and creates an intimate relationship between your physical body, your heart and your Soul.

Feminine ways of knowing speak to me through my subtle energy body in ways that are way beyond the scope of understanding by my logical rational mind.

> *I hear my soul speak as I expand my perceptions of the Invisible realms and I connect to the dimensions of Cosmic Intelligence.*

There is a growing awareness that we have been blessed with two brains, the thinking brain of the mind/logos that we all know and value; and the subtle sensing/psyche brain of the heart. This second is more diffuse and complex for it speaks through all dimensions of our being, and connects us to Cosmic Intelligence in the following ways:

- Psychic Aura ~ Energy Presence
- Inter-Relational Energy of Synastry
- Universal Mind ~ Cosmic Intelligence

Feminine Consciousness is available to us through the intelligence within our energy body. When we consciously choose to let go of the analytical mind, and enter into a place of not knowing this creates the experience of open space. Holding an open space is a crucial step towards entering into the possibility for something new to emerge out of that spaciousness. We can choose where we place our attention and this is where our energy goes.

Heart Intelligence

Body Wisdom

Intuition

Imagination

Psychic Knowing

These five ways of Feminine knowing emerge from inner listening and giving space and time to tune into our subtle energy body.

This allows us to awaken our imagination, our intuition and our psychic knowing, and discover a magical, creative force that is the Heart Intelligence of Soul.

Lets explore these Feminine ways of knowing…..

CHAPTER 10
BODY WISDOM

*Innate Body Wisdom knows instinctively how to heal
and how to create new life*

We need to learn to trust the intelligence of our body's wisdom. Our trust in the outer world grows when we become conscious of the 'What Is' of life, grounded and present to the Earth, and feeling held by Gaia (Mother Earth).

Grounding ~ Earthing ~ Becoming Present

Practical and magical forces combine when we connect to our bodies, the world of nature and the magnetic forces of the earth in each moment in present time.

Notice where you place your energy, for your energy is a precious commodity. How you use your energy impacts upon your life. The quality of your presence effects your magnetic power and influences the intensity of the magic you experience.

Our soul knows the truth of who we are here to become and when this truth is unacknowledged it registers as pain within our bodies. Listening into the body is the first step to uncovering your truth so take a moment to slow down and listen within.

Your body has been telling you a story that you may choose to ignore. Below are phrases to foster enquiry:

1. Where do you feel tension? Where do you feel pain?
2. What valuable message is hidden within your pain?
3. Where do you feel anger? Where do you feel sadness?
4. Is there a deeper message of longing in your heart?
5. What thoughts do you have about your body and what words do you say to yourself?
6. Do you take time to nurture and feed your body?
7. Do you give your body the freedom to express itself and do you listen when your body speaks?
8. How loving are you towards yourself?

Breath Connects us to our Body's Wisdom.

Our in breath feeds and energises us as it travels into our body and at the same time it connects us to the energy of the world around us. It is our out breath that is valuable as a letting go, allowing us to release energy to flow out of the body, preparing us to naturally experience the next slow in breath that follows.

This surrender of the breath is the part that becomes difficult especially when there is tension or excitement in the air. Trauma too can create a habit of holding onto the breath. Fear, mistrust and tension creates this pattern of holding our breath instead of allowing it to flow with a natural rhythm and this holding on robs us of the life giving oxygen our body relies upon and prevents the next new breath to easily arise, creating shallow breathing resulting in a lack of energy.

Working with the breath allows us to relax, slow down and connect more deeply into our body; to feel into our heart, connect with our emotions and nourish our sacred centre as we feed our inner flame.

It takes focused attention to feel into your body and listen into your emotions. When you look beneath your anger you will often find deep sadness that has been masked by your anger and buried emotions that feel too unsafe or vulnerable to ever be acknowledged or brought into the light.

Physical touch and grounding practices, by standing barefoot on the earth, or lying down on the earth to feel the pulse of Gaia (mother earth) can help us to release any built up of stress within our energy body. It becomes so important for us to release energy overloads in our body from the Hi-Tech virtual world we find ourselves living in. Being grounded is being present to your physical energy body, connected to the earth and focused on your breath. This helps to relax your nervous system making it easier for you to fall into a deep sleep at the end of a day.

Your soul wisdom is always there waiting to acknowledged. Slow yourself down into a state of open stillness and aliveness so that you become receptive to subtle messages that speak to you in their own good time.

Know Your Body is in Service to your Soul

CHAPTER 11

HEART INTELLIGENCE

*Discover a magical, creative force
that is the heart intelligence of your soul*

Feminine Intelligence is gained through our perceptions of the Invisible realms. Our task is to synthesis meaning from this 'other' dimension of consciousness.

There is often a sense of mystery to the diffuse and magical forms of subtle information and intuitive guidance.

Heart Intelligence expresses itself in many different ways and it's messages arrive through a variety of experiences:

- Instinct & Emotion
- Body Wisdom
- Intuition
- Psychic Knowing

- Imagination & Dreams
- Inner Child Pre-cognition
- Movement & Dance
- Music & Song

Moving Beyond Fear

An active logos/left brain often works tirelessly to convince us that our limiting thoughts, self criticism and disempowering habits are our truth. However the reality is they hold power over us, limiting our perceptions and prevent us from being able to experience our joy.

- We are taught to value our logical left brain thinking and to mistrust our right brain knowing.
- We believe we must keep the past alive by re-living old memories and focusing on what has been. We fear that if we release our attachment to our memories we will forsake something valuable that will be lost to us forever.
- Our Feminine ways of knowing come from a very different experience of ourselves as a subtle energy body that carries an innate intelligence.

Our task is to bring into consciousness old repeating stories, and to shine a light on strongly held beliefs and outdated thought patterns that hold the power to create self defeating behaviours that often limit our happiness.

The challenge lies in our willingness to go courageously into our heart which is home to our Feminine Intelligence and listen deeply into the bones of our being.
Being willing to enter the depths of our emotional body

becomes a first step in beginning to experience the immense power of love and the deep well of intelligence and love alive within each of us.

Heart Intelligence

Heart energy is an intelligence that reaches far beyond the mind for it speaks to us in the language of the Soul. When we begin to walk the path of the Creatress we set out on a journey that leads us into an intimate connection with our heart's wisdom.

There are simple ways in which we can tune into our inner wise self so that we develop the strength of our connection to this source of intelligence that is innately ours and bring into consciousness an expanded perception of the authenticity of our Soul.

Our happiness depends on finding the courage to journey into our heart, to deepen into our personal truth, and to unearth the gift of our inner gold.

> *Feel into your heart and live from this place of Inner knowing that is your wise and loving Soul.*

Soul Knowing

> *Psyche or Soul is the gestalt of our energy blueprint that energetically expresses the whole of who we are*

Feminine Intelligence is our way of being in touch with body, emotions, imagination, psychic and intuitive consciousness.

Soul is both personal and cosmic. Our personal Soul speaks to us through all of our senses. Being alone in nature has a way of connecting us to the innate wisdom of the earth and the stars.

I have reshaped my world to include the Yin intelligence alive within me. I listen into my heart and hear the messages that arise from this inner place where Love vibrations can be felt. This emotional intelligence speaks to me in the wise and loving voice of my soul.

I have learned to ask clear questions. I take the time to hold questions lightly with my mind and then I let them go. I ask for guidance to come to me while I sleep. In this way I am handing over my problems for unconscious powers to go to work in service of my life.

When I listen into my heart, I hear subtle messages. I have learned to catch these messages and put them outside of myself onto paper as words, colours and images. Sometimes they come to me in a song and I find myself dancing to music that arises from within me.

This is an expression from the creative realms of Yin intelligence that arises out of the depths of my soul and resonates with a loving knowing in my heart.

Be willing to give Love and receive Love
And know that You Are LOVE

CHAPTER 12

INTUITION

*Intuition is Cosmic intelligence that flashes into
our consciousness for brief moments in time.*

Intuition or In-tuition is an inner knowing that comes to us when we slow down and open to hearing our inner voice. This can come as the voice of higher mind, when we tap into the universal intelligence of cosmic consciousness.

Intuition connects us to subtle truths most often as the words of an inner small voice. As you learn to trust in guidance from your intuition, your connection to your feminine intelligence strengthens becoming a knowing that resonates as truth in your heart.

∼

Intuition can arrive like a bolt of lightening out of the blue that awakens us to a new thought form that can leave just as quickly as it arrived. Sometimes it can take time for us to recognise and trust in this inner guidance.

I experience intuition as a deep inner knowing that feels right and true that carries the sense of a calm and peaceful kind of knowingness that shifts my perspective and expands my awareness.

Feminine Intelligence reshapes my world
And reveals my path to finding happiness

Successful leaders, artists and creatives of all kinds have learned to value their intuition and the guidance it brings to them in their everyday lives. They are open to trusting in that small voice that often speaks to them, and through that trust their inner voice becomes clearer and stronger every time.

As a child I remember my mother saying that talking to yourself was the first sign of madness. And yet I find myself holding a conversation with my inner self on a regular basis to tune into my intuitive knowing. It is a primary source of information and a way for me to uncover my inner wisdom.

Inner Listening & Intuition

The simplest of ways is the act of Prayer with eyes wide open. In this way we create a sacred space, we set a clear intention and sit in an open stillness. Just by listening into our inner world we become inner focused and willing to venture into the unknown.

Answers sometimes arrive in the words of a song, or music that feels so right and true, awakening a knowing that was always there, that bring tears of happiness to my eyes.

Rituals that honour the simple truths of nature can open us to this different way of knowing. Patience and the creation of sacred space help to facilitate an awareness of intuitive knowings. Our expanded conscious then empowers us to be able to make better choices.

Sometimes flashes of intuition arrive when least expected, surprising us with simple yet profound guidance.

The more we trust in these subtle whispers the stronger they become as a wise companion on our life's journey.

CHAPTER 13

IMAGINATION

*I*magination is always present in our lives and yet we often do not notice the power it has over us. Our beliefs feed our imagination in ways we may not even notice, especially when we use it to reinforce our fears and magnify our negative emotions.

The artist uses imagination consciously and young children live in a world of active imagination as they explore and play throughout their day creating an intense aliveness and receptiveness to their world.

First allow yourself to believe in a possibility so that it can become real. Creativity is fuelled by our emotions and fed by our imagination. It informs our actions and moves us in the direction of our dreams.

Ancient cultures knew that becoming the dreamer allowed them to tap into the imaginal realms. Dreaming was an important part of alchemy and one of the necessary processes of transformation within the Elysian Mystery experience.

Imagination takes flight in our dreams and if we choose to we can bring it alive in our awakened lucid dreaming as well. Dreams come in many varieties and they speak directly to us, with stories from the unconscious realms that have the power to awaken our ability for image making and stir our inner knowing.

The first steps to being able to create a new life story depends upon how you are using your Imagination. Learning to trust yourself and love your inner world feeds into the way you frame your Intentions. Imagination together with a clear intention creates focused energy. This awakens the power of creativity which colours our thoughts, our dreams and our behaviours.

Used positively imagination ~

- Fuels empowering beliefs
- Opens you to new possibilities
- Enriches your memories of the past
- Expands your vision of the future
- Becomes food for your soul

The science of man and the laws of the universe have been explored for centuries. Now the visible and the invisible realms are meeting in the hearts and minds of mankind, with new philosophies that prescribe ways to bring these realms together. They are calling us to trust numinous moments, they offer us ways to engage our imagination and expand our perceptions of our world and our place in it.

If we can imagine something then it becomes possible to manifest in the physical realms of form. Ground breaking books are opening us to new possibilities ~

> Rupert Sheldrake's *Morphic Resonance: The Nature of Formative Causation*
> Dr. Jo Dispenza's book *Breaking the Habit of Being Yourself: How to lose Your Mind and Create a New One*
> And Bruce Lipton's *The Biology of Belief*

> Take care how you engage with the immense
> power of your imagination. Do not fear the
> darkness of the unknowable realms, Used wisely it
> can illuminate your creative essence that leads you
> along the pathway to your Soul

> Ask yourself ~
> Where am I placing my focus?
> Do I enjoy the results that come from
> the stories I feed with my imagination?

There is power in image and symbol to awaken your imagination. Tarot, Astrology, and symbolic artwork uses symbols and images that are able to elicit psychic awareness and intuitive knowing to arise into consciousness.

This takes creativity to another level allowing your inner child to play and inspiring you with an aliveness that fills your heart with creative passion.

CHAPTER 14

PSYCHIC KNOWING

The word Psychic comes from the Greek *psychilkos* meaning *of the soul* and from *psychē* meaning *soul*.

*P*sychic knowing gives us the ability for telepathy, clairvoyance, or mediumship to channel intelligence from beyond and to know, sense, feel, taste and be present to the energy field of another.

Merrian-Webster dictionary describes Psychic:
Sensitive to non physical or supernatural forces and influences: marked by extraordinary or mysterious sensitivity, perception or understanding.

There are many misconceptions and disbeliefs around this subject of psychic/psyche. Different words used to describe psychic carry very different connotations such as seer, prophet, visionary, clairvoyant, intuitive or mystic.

Psychic abilities can be described as extra sensory perceptions; a sensitive who feels into the energy field of another; A medium who channels intelligence from beyond, who is able to glimpse into a knowledge of the future and connects to spirits of the past.

Which of these descriptions resonate with you? Are you open to receiving in these ways or are you closed and unable to trust that these other ways of knowing are real?

A modern mystic can be thought of as mystical, spiritual, magical, other-worldly, a knowing soul who is informed by emotions, intuition and psychic knowing.

Inner focus, self reflection and subtle ways of sensing can help to raise your energy vibrations. Imagery and emotions are elements of psychic language. It is like becoming a tuning fork as you resonate with energy as it enters into your consciousness.

When you raise your vibrational field to finer levels, this opens you to be able to resonate with subtle energies and sense the colour and sounds of frequencies that are part of a Cosmic consciousness that some can glimpse in numinous moments. Once experienced you are changed forever, there is no going back to an unawakened Soul. Feelings of Loving connectedness remain within the knowing wisdom of your heart.

You become a Sorceress as heightened sensitivity grows and you open to the Cosmic Intelligence from Source

CHAPTER 15

FEMININE PRESENCE

Feminine Essence is primal feminine energy
the Yin intelligence of who you are
the raison d'être of your soul

Your presence has the power to change the world with the resonance of magnetic forces that are expressions of your truth. Magnetism is an energy force that emanates from within. It effects all who come into the presence of this powerful feminine force and synchronicities occur to shout out to us when we are on our Soul path.

Live a Life of Soul
Sing your songs of love
Awaken the beauty in your heart
For it is this truth that heals your soul
A truth that is gracious, loving and kind
Align your physical presence with your soul
Embrace the dance of life as magical mystery
Learn to flow as one and live in the river of Love

A Creatress has developed trust in her creative energy and she knows the quality of her presence is the source of her soul power.

Eight lessons of a Creatress go together in pairs

Listening ~ Trusting
Feeling ~ Being
Imagining ~ Knowing
Sensing ~ Attuning

It takes courage to walk the path of a Creatress. When you do, you learn how to live creatively in every moment and your life unfolds before you with elegance and grace.

Become the presence of the Creatress, step into your Feminine power and claim your Authenticity.

When we are aligned to our soul purpose we feel joy arise spontaneously from within and our light body shines with the quality of our presence.

Signs of being in alignment with soul ~

- Spontaneous singing
- Feelings of enthusiasm on waking
- Willingness to imagine a positive future
- Joy that arises just from being alive
- Openness to unfolding patterns of living
- Synchronicities abound

- Feelings of clarity, peace and harmony
- Connect to a bigger picture, a world of possibility

Go with the natural flow of energy and learn to trust in your inner wisdom as it guides you on your journey to becoming a joyful, loving and creative soul.

Creativity arises out of the invisible realms
as you become a channel and flow with unfolding
mystery creating expressions of cosmic intelligence.

I have come to know her feminine power by re-owning the unacknowledged gifts of my feminine intelligence. This has led me to become open, receptive and sensitive to the subtle realms of my personal soul's knowing and the innate wisdom I have gained through my experiences of living, loving and being fully present in the physical realm.

This inner journey leads you to connect to your feminine intelligence, to heal any wounds alive in your heart and uncover the knowing wisdom of your soul. This is the true essence of the heroine's journey, to come home to the presence and power of your virgin self.

She lives in the river of love and
flows in tune with the music of her soul

PART IV

THE YIN INTELLIGENCE OF HEART

Learn to Trust the Feminine Intelligence within you …..

A LOVE TOKEN

Follow your knowing for this changes who you become
Choose wisely and listen for the sound of your own drum

Be courageous, take heart and hear the angels sing
Blessed be and blessed all, as you become a ring
The feminine is a circle that cannot be broken
A symbol of your soul's gift, a love token

There is rhythm and a music that is your song
Learn to hear it call you as you dance along
Being in the flow, with nowhere else to go
Oh what joy for your true self to show

The brighter your soul's light glows
The lighter your warm heart flows
Loving the beauty that is you
Comes from being real and true

Love begins with you
Share it too

CHAPTER 16

THE WOUNDED HEART

*T*he heroine's journey becomes a quest that leads you into your heart to heal any wounds and connect into the intelligence of your Feminine Essence. Heart Intelligence is an energy that reaches far beyond the mind for it speaks to us in the language of our Soul.

There is much needed for the healing of a wounded heart that happens at the dimension of soul. Until you develop a mature and loving relationship with your self, and a knowing connection to the wisdom of your soul, only then are you able to shine your light and share your love in the world. When we restore our ability to truly love ourselves, we also nurture and heal our Soul.

Trauma Happens, it is part of the human experience. Even the act of birthing may be fraught with dangers that some do not survive.

As we travel on this journey of Becoming we garner a wealth of experiences that include the wounding of the heart and a sadness of the soul. This breaking open of the heart is part of the human experience that few are able to avoid.

Into the Shadowlands

Trauma occurs when something happens that breaks us open and forces us to step outside of our comfort zone and leave our old world behind.

We enter a transition zone, a no man's land of not knowing, a Neptunian world of the shadowlands. Feelings of confusion, loss and grief for what is no more consume us as we fall into a dark space of deep despair.

Our inner light begins to fade, our energy vibrations lessen and we no longer feel or know who we are. This painful place of not knowing can lead us down into a spiral of deep despair. Our perceptions dim and distortions reign. Our old self appears to be lost to us and we feel overwhelmed by unknown challenges that lie ahead.

Old Smokey Lens

We view our lives through an old smokey lens that is based upon old imaginings that are clouded by mistrust and fear. We close our hearts and carry around the heavy weight of painful memories. At some point our lives come to a standstill, we pause and then we begin to question ourselves and seek new answers to the disappointments in our lives.

CHAPTER 17

HEALING THE HEART

Heal your Heart ~ Hear your Soul

For me healing is whole making and most often it requires healing the heart and the emotional body in such a way that we become able to validate the presence of our Yin intelligence.

If you have loved you will always carry that love within you, if you have been loved this can never be taken away from you, your heart remembers always.

It takes time and sacred space to allow the subconscious realms to process the intensity of our life's experiences, especially when we are going through transformational times both externally and internally. Down time and open ended dream time combined with gentleness and loving kindness create the sacred space needed for rest and relaxation for the process of healing to unfold.

Your heart may have cracks and may have died a little at times. When we become willing to surrender all of our hurts and allow our heart to open, to feel and be vulnerable again, this awakens us to our loving and playful inner child.

It is time for you to re-member that you are a Soul Star, a child of the Universe. You are connected to the invisible realms, the subtle knowings, and the great mystery.

You are a multi-dimensional being grounded in a physical form and you are here to experience the unfolding of the immense creativity and magical power that unveils the empowered presence of your sacred Soul.

Healing the Heart

The ability to heal ourselves is a force alive within each of us. First we must address old stuck grief that has lodged as memory stored within our body, and sometimes even in our bones.

A heart that is closed carries the heavy weight of painful memories. It is full of grief that has settled in the body, weighting you down, sapping your energy and removing experiences of joy from your life.

To heal the heart and hear the Soul we are asked to connect deeply into ourselves and feel into the gestalt of our whole body experience.

Preparing for the Journey into your Heart

- Value physical presence in time and space.
- Listen into the calling of your Soul
- Open your heart and surrender old wounds
- Honour the mystery and experience the magic

- Bath yourself in the magnetic forces of Love
- Give yourself a sacred space in which to heal
- Be gentle and loving towards your secret self

Finding Inner Strength

Life will test us, our experiences make us learn and grow and our wisdom comes from knowing we can make wise choices and over time we strengthen our trust in our inner guidance.

I think of my heart as if it were a piece of Kintsugi pottery. It has been broken at times and cracks have appeared in its form, so it will never again contain only the innocent pure wonder and perfection of the heart of a new born.

Kintsugi is the ancient Japanese art form of mending pottery that has been broken by joining the pieces back together with strands of molten gold. A vase that is weaved together with strands of gold becomes stronger and more beautiful than ever before. It becomes an original work of art valued for its uniqueness and its authentic beauty with its own exquisite and unique complexity.

We all carry wounds in our hearts. We need to find the courage to mend our heart back together. These wounds and experiences of our past have moulded and shaped us into who we have become. It is these experiences that humanise us and give us our ability to perceive both empathy and compassion for the human experience.

Transformation of Heart

Life has brought me challenges that have created a depth of emotions and a plethora of experiences that are the stuff of my becoming.

Transformation begins when we break open our heart to set the beauty and truth of our soul free. Behind the scenes the alchemy of soul and the pure essence of creativity are at work awakening our authenticity that is at the core of our being, only then can we truly heal.

Transformation happens in its own time, it cannot be rushed or forced into becoming. It's process requires that we bravely enter into the hidden parts of ourself, to witness stories we believe in. They hold a power over us that creates our reality.

The more you trust in yourself this opens you to experiences of the Feminine power within you and awareness of a different kind of intelligence that comes from your Soul.

Living from the Heart

Healing the heart comes from letting go of fears and learning to trust in a higher intelligence that can only be received when there is openness and warmth in your heart.

To know the truth alive within us requires that we become receptive to intuitive wisdom and be guided by the wise intelligence of our Feminine knowing.

When we truly love ourself, then we become real ~ a unique authentic soul. Healing the heart becomes the way into a life of Soulful joyousness. It is our heart's energy that radiates our magnetic presence. Like magnetically attracts like.

How grounded are you?

It is crucial that we become well grounded and accepting of our human experiences to become a conscious channel for our soul. Feet placed firmly on the earth, become one with the world of nature, draw energy up from the earth and down from the stars and reach out to the community of souls around you.

Connected to your body, sensing your aura, feeling into your heart, listening to your thoughts, processing with your gut, and focusing on your sacred centre.

Healing the heart is the key to unlocking your truth buried deep within. Only when we fully accept ourself with all our missteps and foibles and all our imperfections can we begin to live authentically in alignment with our soul.

Our life becomes a work of art as we mend our wounds and reshape our stories into something that is unique and unrepeatable and reflects the true essence of our Soul.

When we go beyond the programming of our rational mind and enter into the spaciousness between our thoughts, only then can we uncover the wealth of intelligence that is freely available to us all. It cannot be defined, controlled, commercialised or predicted. It is in this space between where magic happens.

There is a growing body of humans who are connecting into the Cosmic intelligence that surrounds us. It speaks in a Universal language that has the beauty and simplicity of a mathematical equation and the grace of a dancer.

When you heal your heart, you heal your soul
You begin to live a life of joyful creativity

CHAPTER 18
HEART WISDOM

The core essence of the Feminine is Creativity
Her search for meaning becomes a search
for the Aliveness of a Loving Heart

This is something that comes naturally to us when two souls meet, there is a feeling of coming home that we have longed for, a sense of safety and a comfort, and a sense that it is ok to show our authentic self to another.

The challenge is to become present to ourself in this same manner which requires that we give ourselves permission just to be fully present to self in a kind and loving way.

We all carry memories of times when our hearts have been damaged and our emotions have felt too overwhelming to be fully embraced. Over time we close down, hide our true emotions and feel too unsafe to ever reveal our truth to others. We may experience shame, hurt and fear the beliefs we hold about ourselves and so we hide our most vulnerable self from others. In so doing we limit our ability to experience intimacy and the soul closeness that we long for. When we learn how to open our heart and feel the warmth of its inner glow we find there is no longer room for fear to exist.

Your soul creates a magnetic energy force which emanates from your heart and reaches out into your aura. This energy field created by your open and loving heart has a truth and beauty to it that can be sensed by others and they will in turn mirror this energy back to you.

Others will feel the essence of your soul and resonate with its warmth or be repelled by it if they are unwilling or unready to accept this energy presence within their own soul.

The aim becomes to heal your heart and hear your Soul as you trust in the messages that come to you and live creatively, guided by your Feminine Intelligence.

Re-member you are a manifestation of Source
~ a unique and unrepeatable soul.

Part of the process is to rediscover the child within and to embrace that playful, innocent part of ourselves. This is an act of truly loving ourselves just as we are. As you observe the What Is of your life you become Real and True. Becoming real takes time, as we peel away the false beliefs and values not in alignment with our authentic soul essence.

This becoming real is described beautifully in the beloved children's story of *The Velveteen Rabbit*

> "Real isn't how you are made"
> said the skin horse,
> "it's a thing that happens to you.
>
> When a child loves you for a
> long time, not just to play with
> but Really loves you,
>
> then you become Real."
>
> The Velveteen Rabbit
> Margery Williams

Feminine Mystery and Magic

When you learn to tap into the mystery and magic of your feminine wise self, you become empowered to make new choices and become infused with the passion, beauty and grace that comes from your soul.

> *The secret to true happiness comes from living*
> *Creatively and authentically in every moment,*
> *Uncover your gifts and share them in the world*
> *From a place of loving kindness and grace.*

Each Soul is surrounded by an aura of authentic inner light that is the illumined glow of their Soul. They are a unique expression of Cosmic Source here on earth.

As you awaken the presence of your inner self, you come to know that you are the Wisdom Keeper of your Soul

Go deep within and ask yourself ~ *"Who am I?"*
Your soul knows the answer to your question
A Sacred ~ Heart Centred ~ Soul

Emotional intelligence

The intensity of your emotions, are not there to overpower you but to inform you from the depths of your instinctual emotional body.

Emotions are a felt experience that reverberates within the body and resonates within the heart. They are the carriers of important information that needs to be felt to begin to be understood. They are the messengers of body wisdom and in particular the wisdom of your heart.

Water is the element associated with emotions describing the quality of energy that moves as a circle, a spiral, and a wave that flows forever morphing into new patterns. The waters of the earth flow like a river across the land bringing life-giving elements. So too does the water within your body bring passion and aliveness to you through your emotions.

Without trust there is mistrust which is based upon our perceptions often distorted by the emotions of fear. While there is fear and mistrust in the air there can be no experience of Love. The one cancels out the other.

Emotions are vibrations of pure energy and every emotion has its own vibrational frequency that is unique to you. The inner knowing from your Soul has a resonance that feels right and true for you.

Place your energy into that which you wish to bring alive in your life. Be guided by the emotional language of your soul calling you to follow your heart. Your heart will lead you into places and experiences you could not have imagined. You then discover that you are limited only by your own imagination.

Living from the Heart

There is no room for fear or mistrust to arise when you live with love in your heart. This energy that trusts you to be Real is the energy of authenticity that reaches out to others and touches into their souls. It is through this energy of your open heart that you connect to the great ocean of Cosmic love. Feel yourself being buoyed up and supported as you relax into a place of safety within yourself, floating on the Ocean of life

> When you are able to define clear boundaries then you are able to reclaim your power, until then you will find yourself giving your power away to others. Clear boundaries define what is or is not ok for you, they give you the power to develop trust within yourself; so you can live in the flow, deciding each day to take small steps in the direction of your dreams.

When you live with the warmth of an open heart you find yourself sharing your gifts with others. This then becomes the simple unfolding of the creative process and Magic begins to happen.

When you dream big, believe your dream is possible and feel truly ready to receive this dream this is when the universe conspires to bring your dream alive with the surprise of magic.

When you let go of your need to grieve for your past, for nothing is ever truly lost, this is a first step to imagining a New World into Becoming.

You will find yourself feeling true to yourself, doing what you really love and enjoying the freedom to soar into the beyond. The warmth in your heart creates an energy that uplifts all who enter your space and you experience a world that is way beyond the limited imagination of the old thinking of your past.

It takes bravery and courage together with a dollop of passion to begin a new story, to engage in new challenges, explore new possibilities and stay open to a new direction.

This is how magic happens as you trust in your inner voice, risk taking with a small step in a new direction and be open to a different story unfolding. Small steps over time lead to big dreams coming true.

Your heart is the barometer of your soul. You are energy vibrating in time and space, and you are sending your unique energy frequency into the world. When you change your frequency you change your life, with new thoughts and beliefs you can change your world.

The Creatress Way is a graceful dance between two worlds, to know the eternal wisdom in your soul and to feel the love and truth alive within your heart with the Presence of a Creatress.

Being present to your inner world and the subtle energies that reside there and awake to the outer world and present to this moment. You are living authentically from your heart.

New thought, ancient wisdom and the simplicity of authenticity becomes the unfolding journey home to your essential self.

*Heart Wisdom brings the beauty, grace, peace,
and power of Creatress Magic into Your World*

PART V
THE GREAT MYSTERY

Into the darkness to meet the magnetic forces within …..

WOMB MAGIC

*The ultimate creation source of all humankind
Is the dark wisdom of womb magic
That nurtures all new life*

*This darkness is the dimension where
Potentiality and Creativity catalyse the
Miracle of manifesting into new forms*

CHAPTER 19

FORM AND FORMLESSNESS

Form and formlessness has a space in-between that is the transition place where alchemy is possible.

This time and space of waiting as the old falls away and the new is not yet formed can be a place where feelings of loss and sadness arise, impatience and confusion too.

To be able to manifest a new life begins with this process of unfolding and releasing old forms and ways of being.

The transition phase of any birthing process can be the most painful place to be, where all that has been is dissolving into pure essence and fear arises for all that is being lost and for the unknown that is yet to be.

This is the cocoon phase of waiting and not knowing that cannot be skipped in any transformational experience. There is a timing to the unfolding, of that which is unknown which cannot be rushed, all you can do is wait in trust with an open heart.

Awareness of feelings of loss of identity, confusion and sadness are sure signs that the power of alchemy is at work within you. This carries the implicit promise of something new yet to come.

We must be willing to own the stories we tell ourselves and the messages that we believe to be true, and to become conscious of our repeating patterns that create repeating outcomes.

So often someone who has achieved amazing results in their life will tell their story of believing in their vision from an early age. They held a dream within them and never let it go. Sometimes they speak of luck or someone believing in them who held a torch to help light their path. This always helps but it comes back to the ability to hold a dream in their heart and to never let it go.

The power of this clarity of intention cannot be understated. When a calling comes from the heart, it is a direct message from soul not to be ignored.

CHAPTER 20

CHAOS & CREATIVITY

*W*omb Magic happens behind the scenes in darkness and creativity includes both committed effort and the playful magic of child like wonder as we embrace creativity as the Art of Becoming.

Space to go into the chaos, to loosen the structures that have given meaning, to let go of the known and to wait in the darkness. This waiting becomes an incubation period that gives time for Cosmic Intelligence to do its work.

Creativity begins in the unseen realms of darkness and evolves out of experiences and the willingness to flow as life unfolds with trust in the knowing that something new is about to emerge.

The Dark Feminine carries the energy of the primal forces of the great mother. Her power is magnetic energy.

She can be likened to the negative charge at the South Pole, this place found opposite the North Pole which carries the positive charge. She is negative only in the sense of magnetic power, she is aligned with the mystery of the great attractor, the magnetic force at the core of the earth.

> *To know her is to overcome your fear of the unknown*
> *The darkness and the depths of your emotions.*
> *Know the longing in your heart as the magnetic*
> *Mystery of your soul that calls to you*

Creativity requires that we make many small choices, and discover through the processes of experiencing, learning and growing. It may begin with the spark of an idea and requires perseverance and courage to bring that initial essence into a new form.

Creation is an unfolding process that evolves out of the experiences themselves. Synchronicities are a sign you are on the path of an awakening Soul.

> *Allow life's creative processes to unfold*
> *Practical and magical mysteries combine*
> *And you become more than you ever*
> *Imagined your self to be*

Foster your ability to give yourself permission to enter into the chaos and hold the tension to allow something new to emerge.

Patience, giving the time necessary for mystery to unfold and take form.
Intention, to believe in a new possibility.
Imagination, becomes the passion that feeds creativity.
Trust, allowing energy to flow with its own rhythm and timing.

- The Creative Process requires patience and trust.
- It has its own timing and will not be rushed.
- There is a knowing in the waiting, that something as yet unknowable is forming.
- It takes ingredients and synthesises them into something totally new.

As any artist knows it is a delicate combination of effort and dedication together with the ability to flow with the spirit of playful childlike wonder. Over time we expand our capacity to hold higher energy frequencies of cosmic intelligence that are freely available to each of us.

CHAPTER 21

DARKNESS AND LIGHT

> *I am mystery unfolding out of darkness,*
> *I am the Black Virgin and the Black Madonna*
> *I personify the powers contained within darkness*
> *I believe in the creative forces of my beloved child*
> *My invisibility is a necessary part of*
> *My mystery and my magic*

The denigration and disempowerment of the feminine by the patriarchal culture we know so well with its needs to control and have power over nature, has resulted in the rape of our lands and the rape of our women. By re-owning the power of the wise dark feminine we awaken our creative power to birth new ways, that are so badly needed in todays crazy world.

Our fear of darkness and our projection of evil onto that darkness is just another expression of this denigration of the Feminine and the domination of the Masculine that creates many limiting false beliefs that we unconsciously chose to live by.

Only when we are willing to make friends with the dark mystery of the Feminine can we begin to heal the imbalance between the Masculine and the Feminine and enrich our lives with magic and mystery.

Into the Darkness

> *Find your light that glows from within the darkness*
> *Your inner light is where you connect into the*
> *pure essence of your sacred flame.*

Develop an intimate relationship with yourself and live a life rich in creative consciousness as you honour the lightness and darkness within. We need to appreciate them both for they are interconnected polarities of the same matrix.

> Alchemy meaning *black earth* is the process of whole making and the essence of dark creative power.

> This inner darkness holds a dimension of potentiality of the magic to manifest energy into new forms.

> The dark moon phase is a necessary part of the cycle that gives time for us to rest and nurture new seeds of creativity, within the safety of the dark womb.

A willingness to enter the dark mystery realms, is to enter into a space of chaos and potentiality. This place deep inside of you is a sacred place where magic happens and you become conscious of the aliveness of yourself as soul.

When you become one with this inner space, you discover the key to aligning with your truth and you connect to the vast creative potentiality from Source.

Persephone and the Black Madonna are archetypal expressions of the ancient primal force of the dark feminine. They know the mystery unfolding out of darkness, they see into the truth of a soul and know how to express the magic of Feminine Essence.

The Black Virgin represents
the pure essence of feminine power
Like a well-spring of purest water that
arises from a place deep within the earth.

Creativity is the core of her essential self
A fountain of an immense power that
connects her to the intelligence of Source.

She loves her darkness and her inner glow,
for they are expressions of her Becoming
the consciousness of her awakened Soul.
Our loving relationship to her darkness
is the energy that heals our hearts.

A Persephone woman shape shifts between two worlds. She is at home with both lightness and darkness. She knows they are complimentary opposites that need each other to be able to exist.

> *Persephone is a modern mystic who willingly*
> *embraces the intelligence of her soul.*

Persephone's underworld is the soul's domain where she accompanies souls as they transition from the physical world. Her inner glow becomes a beacon of light for Souls to follow as they transition back into the freedom and lightness of Cosmic Soul consciousness.

Persephone guides you to reclaim your Feminine Wisdom and know the hidden gifts of your soul.

> *She gives herself permission to shine her light*
> *And to withdraw her light into the realms of darkness*
> *To renew herself in honour of the cycles of becoming*
> *Which are the core of her creative essence*

CHAPTER 22
WOMB MAGIC

The ultimate creation source of all humankind is the dark wisdom of the womb that nurtures all new life

The potentiality of pure energy contains the power to morph into a myriad of different forms, its possibilities remain limitless. This power to Create has recognisable processes and steps to be taken and yet in its essence it remains a mystery. There is an element of surprise and magic inherent in every creative process of alchemy that happens within the darkness.

A Creatress finds her power in the elements of Earth and Water which relate to her grounded Presence and her Emotional Intelligence. Her magnetic Presence, her Passion and her Promise are qualities needed for creativity from within the dark womb to unfold.

∽

Wisdom Keepers are the Goddesses Hestia, Hecate and the mature Persephone who know the power of womb magic.

They are comfortable in the dark realms and sacred spaces where magic happens. They are healers who hold the key to heart vibrations that can heal every wounded heart.

Their innate intelligence makes them wise carriers of the sacred flame of Feminine Essence as a symbol of the creative passion of your inner truth. They do not fear the darkness for they have ventured into the depths of the shadowlands and returned with wisdom that has been gathered from their experiences.

Wisdom Keepers know how to ask the right questions and they have developed deep trust in their inner knowing. They guide you to find the hidden treasure that is the pure gold of your soul's essence and awaken the sacred passion of your Hestia flame. They are archetypal carriers of Soul wisdom and they have experienced the alchemy of rebirth into a life of soul consciousness.

A wisdom Keeper can guide you to find your light that glows from within darkness where you connect into the pure essence of your Sacred Soul. Live from this place of feminine knowing, trust your wise and loving heart and know you are a unique and unrepeatable soul.

Go into the darkness to find your inner light
This is the key to unlock the secret to finding your joy

PART VI
ANCIENT FEMININE ARCHETYPES

When You Choose to Say *Yes* to Yourself …..

PERSEPHONE'S DANCE

*She moves elegantly through her
world with simplicity and grace
Her inner glow lights her way
A quiet calm upon her face*

*She listens to words
that are not spoken and
Hears songs not being sung
Her emotions and her instincts
Have become her trusted friends*

*She dances with joy in her heart
Catching whispers from her soul
She journeys into the darkness
Guiding souls when they are lost*

*She is Queen of the Underworld
She emanates a magnetic power
She is at one with the stars and
The Cosmos is her eternal home*

CHAPTER 23
ANCIENT GODDESSES

*A*ncient Goddesses make up the fabric of our past. They remind us of memories from a forgotten time and re-awaken us to subtle facets of our Feminine wisdom. Greek Goddesses are awaking aspects that have been hidden away and forgotten parts that have become lost to us. They are calling each of us in their own way to live creatively from our hearts and embrace the immense power of our Yin Intelligence.

Maiden Goddesses

Psyche is the story of a beautiful maiden who after a journey of love and then loss begins a long journey alone until she is reunited with Eros (true love) and takes her place as an immortal Goddess.

Kore who was later renamed Persephone was abducted into the underworld by Hades, She experiences a loss of innocence and begins to grow into her Feminine power as she becomes Persephone, Queen of the Underworld.

Soul-Making Goddesses

Persephone matures into a woman who lives guided by her subtle senses and her inner knowing in communion with the sacredness of her soul. She is a Goddess of who has empathy and understanding of the (psyche) soul journey. She is the Queen of the Underworld and wife to Hades and she becomes a guide to lost souls. She shines her light in the darkness to assist Souls as they transition between the upper world and the under world on their journey between the dimensions of personal and Cosmic Soul.

Demeter is the Earth goddess of fertility and the Goddess of nature's cycles of death and rebirth. She is mother to Persephone and she is the archetypal Mother Goddess deeply connected to Gaia/Earth and its seasons. Persephone & Demeter are a daughter/mother story of love and loss.

Demeter has known the grief of loss and the joy of her daughters return from the Underworld. Mother and daughter reunite in spring and summer to honour the seasons of rebirth and the return of growth and fertility for six months of every year.

Together they became the founders of The Elysian Mystery School, where they guided people from all walks of life who became initiates, into a self reflective experiential and transformational journey into a life of awakened soul consciousness.

The myth of Persephone and Demeter was told in *The Sacred Dance of Soul*

Hestia is the forgotten Goddess of Sacred Space and keeper of the Sacred Flame. She is also a Virgin Goddess meaning '*she is one unto her self.*' A Greek Goddess and Priestess who tended the fire that burned at the centre of the temple. This flame represented the sacred centre and so it was important that it was kept alive as an eternal symbol of the soul of the city.

Hecate is the Goddess of the Crossroads. She is a wise guide who has the ability to help us make empowering choices especially when we are experiencing times of transition. She becomes midwife to souls in the Underworld in Persephone's absence, when in spring and summer she visits her mother Demeter. Hecate is comfortable in the realms of the earth mysteries, the underworld journey and her connection to the cosmos.

There are many competing sub personalities within each of us and some of their stories describe the tensions inherent within the repeating stories of our lives. These tensions can become a catalyst to create change, and to bring about an inner desire to reinvent ourselves. Let's take a closer look at two Archetypes from book I in the Creatress Magic Series.

Psyche

With the loss of her illusionary idyllic life, she journeys alone and faces many challenges to find her inner strength before she is rewarded with true love and she is given Goddess status as an immortal soul. Psyche is the Goddess of relationship, the experience of true love and our heart's awakening to the presence of our immortal soul.

Black Virgin (La Vierge Noire) is the Dark Feminine who is virgin unto her self. She is both Darkness and Light. She knows how to renew her virgin self and she sees into the truth and beauty within you. She is the Primordial Dark Feminine and her knowing presence sees into the sacredness of your soul.

The myths of Psyche and the Black Virgin are told in *The Odyssey of a Creatress*

Like the Black Virgins, Persephone sees into the truth that lies hidden beneath the surface. These Goddesses are known to be the protectress of women in child birth, and all those who find themselves to be outsiders in society. They arrive when called upon to give direction through the mediums of dreams, intuition, heart knowing and through altered states such as mediation and vision quests. They have the ability to see into the past, the present and the future, and guide you to choose wisely and learn to live in alignment with your soul.

CHAPTER 24

STORIES WE TELL OURSELVES

Do you find yourself living in a world crammed full of old memories?

Old stories create a rich tapestry that colour our human experience with memories of both pain and joy. These stories of the past have a habit of creating our reality. It is highly probable that many of the stories we tell ourselves are disempowering and blatantly untrue. This includes the many stories that shape our fundamental beliefs of who we are.

Old stories are often based upon old beliefs and old programs we run without question. As we listen to these stories, we discover that often they are motivated by fears and doubts together with an array of limiting beliefs and often they are cruel rather than kind.

What if you let your memories go ~ to fade into a distant past of *'what has been'* and then choose to keep only the very best of them *La Creme de la Creme* as companions on your journey.

It is a challenge in today's new world, to re-own our innate creative essence and to go beyond our fears to reclaim our essential Feminine nature. This is the Heroine's journey, to find the courage to become a Creatress of your unique soul story and assert your feminine power.

> *To own your feminine intelligence is to claim your creative power, to love yourself as you are and embrace the beauty of your soul.*

To create a new story begins with unearthing the old stories that have been guiding your life until now. These stories may have been alive within you for so long that often you are not even aware of their presence. Sometimes they originated from a message of a parent or another person of power in your younger life.

Their purpose may have been to protect you, however they may no longer serve you now. Often these stories sap our confidence and become the reason we choose to keep ourselves small so as to keep 'the peace' and not upset others or disrupt the status quo.

If you know in your heart that you are not living in alignment with your personal truth then now is the time to question the memories and old habits of your past, even though they may be comfortably familiar and have helped to shape the person you have become.

It takes courage to let go of old stories, beliefs and habits, and old patterns of behaviour from the past.

To do so is to open your heart and begin to create a new story, one that is aligned to the beauty of your Soul.

Ask yourself ~
"Does this story resonate with the truth in my heart and the beauty of my Soul?"

CHAPTER 25

PERMISSION, CROSSROADS AND CHOICES

Many societies today still honour Patriarchal values and worship the scientific approach as their way of governance and control over their communities.

The centuries old denigration of the Feminine by a culture based upon patriarchy desires to control and have power over both women and nature has resulted in the rape of our lands and the rape of our women. As a result we have learned to mistrust our emotions, ignore our intuitive knowing and deny the power of our Yin Intelligence.

Many of us have learned to look outside of ourselves for answers believing that authority figures are wise and able to decide that which is best for us.

We choose to believe in the stories that others tell us rather than hearing the truth alive within our hearts and we limit the power that our imagination has to be able to enrich the quality of our lives.

This has resulted in a culture where we not only mistrust our Feminine Intelligence, we disowned our soul's wisdom. We need to come into alignment with our heart to be able to live from an intentional place of Soul consciousness.

Permission

Permission is a powerful force, that once given can change the way we feel about ourselves. This begins with giving ourselves permission to value the feminine ways of being which requires that we allow ourselves the time and space to listen into our inner world.

I no longer allow myself to focus on my problems, I withdraw my attention away from them and I choose to place my energy on my vision of possibility.

Permission to let go of old stories and the beliefs we hold about our world and the people in it does not come naturally to many of us.

Permission to place our focus on that which is important to our Soul;

Permission to place value on the emotional resonance of the heart and the instinctual knowing of the body as an act of empowerment.

Give yourself permission to make new choices and imagine fresh new ideas into being and most of all give permission to be loving and kind to yourself.

Perspective

When we climb to the top of a mountain and look into the beyond, we gain an expanded perspective of ourselves in relation to our world.

If the feminine is to take her place beside the masculine as an equal, honouring her essential essence at the core of her being-ness, then she must claim her powers that are so different to the masculine expressions of power. Women have been encouraged to disown their power, hiding it so as to not draw attention to themselves, staying in the shadows, often feeling dissatisfied and disempowered. When we validate the Feminine way of perceiving, this allows us to change of sense of ourselves and find a new place for ourselves in the outer world.

In the Flow

A Creatress is able to be flexible because she is not attached to the outcome, she is willing to be surprised by the creative process. Just like a river that flows into the shape of the land, she is able to meld into the invisible realms and expand her consciousness to perceive more and comprehend a bigger picture.

Being in the flow is to dance with the energies of the moment with an alive state of anticipation towards a fluid and unknowable outcome, so opposite to the fixed determination of logos/rational mind thinking and doing.

A Creatress spends time in nature connecting to the world around her. She knows how to make something that is greater than the sum of its parts. Empower the archetype of the Creatress within you and step into your life as an artist, a mystic and sacred soul.

The power that lives within

The words *feminine* and *power* do not sit easily together. The word empowered seems more meaningful when applied to the feminine. Women of power... powerful women... the power of emotions... psychic power... and the immense power of soul wisdom can sound uncomfortable and unfamiliar to our ears.

I have found that only I can walk my soul path and uncover the power that lives within me; and only you can claim your feminine power by having the courage to honour your heart as you take the journey into your Soul. As you live guided by your Feminine Intelligence you also become receptive to the intelligence of the Cosmos.

> Psychic and Psychology derive from the word psyche meaning soul and Psychic knowing registers as soul messages in subtle ways.
>
> Feminine ways of knowing involve all of the senses. Some are instant and others can take time for their messages to percolate slowly into our emotional body, revealing their meaning to us.
>
> Sensitivity is seen by many to be a weakness and yet it is our sensitivity that gifts us with a sense of closeness and empathy as we enter into intimate relationships and deeper connections that move us way beyond the scope of our rational mind.

There is magic and mystery to this other way of being that gives time and space for us to grow in awareness and sensitivity to our Feminine ways of knowing. They register within our body, mind and heart as somatic, intuitive and psychic messages. Their guidance is the pathway to claiming the magical powers of a Creatress.

Crossroads & Choices

We all have choices but often we are so close to our problems that we are unable to step back and see that we have the right to say Yes or No to what ever is presented to us.

So often we choose to identify with our problem by giving it a label and making it our central focus, and sometimes it becomes our *raison d'être* (reason for living.)

We have the choice to be a victim of our circumstances or to consciously choose to step into a place of personal empowerment.

Maturity happens when we become willing to make our own choices and take responsibility for their outcomes. This is an important step along the path to self realisation that Jung defined as *Individuation* in 1930's. He knew that becoming able to self reflect and see a bigger picture gives us the perspective needed to be able to make empowering choices that are aligned with the calling of our Soul. He saw his life's task as the *'Cure of Souls.'*

We need to give ourselves Permission to recognise when we are at a Crossroads; to be able to step back and gain a wider perspective and to know we hold the power within us to make wise choices create a new experience and begin a new story.

Intention

Withdraw your intention away from all that has been: old stories, old wounds and memories of the past. Make a conscious choice to set a new intention to create a new story.

Old stories have created a rich tapestry that colour our human experience with memories of pain and joy. It takes courage to let go of these old stories, beliefs, habits and old patterns of behaviour from the past and to open your heart to create your unique story, one that is aligned to the beauty of your Soul.

New stories arise out of a Soul perspective as we embrace the invisible realms and bring alive the Feminine archetypes of the Artist, the Modern Mystic and the Creatress.

The secret to true happiness comes from living authentically and creatively in every moment

PART VII
NEW STORIES ~ NEW ARCHETYPES

Love yourself, create your unique story and

Embrace the power of your Feminine Essence .....

CHILD OF THE UNIVERSE

You are a child of the Universe
A soul star of the night sky
So love yourself as you are
Sacred Creatress of cosmic love

Become the unique soul star
You were born to be
Shine your inner light
A golden glow for all to see

So listen deeply and hear
the voice of your soul calling
Trust in your inner wise soul
And feel it's warmth within

Know the music in your heart
And sing your songs of Love
Learn to dance a sacred dance
And let yourself flow with grace

You are a child of the Universe
A singular expression of soul
A manifestation from Source
And vibrations of 'All That Is'

CHAPTER 26

NEW ARCHETYPES

Feminine Essence is Your Creative Power

There are many Ancient Archetypes being reborn and empowering new Archetypes arising into consciousness with the power to enliven the presence of empowered Feminine Essence.

Let's take a look at new Feminine Archetypes making their presence felt in todays world.

Creatress
Modern Mystic
Mature Persephone
Soul Star ~ Cosmic Child
La Femme ~ Feminine Essence

New Feminine Archetypes

New Feminine Archetypes bring forth the possibility to re-imagine our lives and begin to create a new world. The challenge is to find your way into a story that mirrors the magnificence of your authentic self and the innate gifts you are here to share with the world.

The Creatress, Modern Mystic and Soul Star are archetypes to harness the power of our inner light and awaken the presence of feminine soul within us all. They carry the Essence of what has been before and awaken the presence of the new empowered Feminine to come.

Let yourself feel into the warmth of your heart, connect to your sacred inner flame; listen and hear the voice of your Feminine Intelligence. Then you will find that you have gained the ability to live a life filled with passion and joy.

The Creatress

> *A Creatress dances between the visible and invisible realms*
> *She values darkness as fertile ground for creative inspiration.*

A Creatress is the archetype of the Creative Woman. Creatress is both an Alchemical Goddess and Modern Mystic who understands transformational mysteries.

She is a Maker of New Life and her creativity arises out of her passion and her power to create new stories.

The feminine body knows instinctively how to create new life. Our Feminine Essence knows how to create our truely authentic soul story.

A Creatress is also a shapeshifter who moves fluidly between two worlds. The ways of a Creatress are Simplicity, Honesty, Open Listening and Heart Centred living.

She has developed an unwavering trust in her feminine intelligence and her life unfolds with ease and grace.

Becoming conscious of her soul's presence comes naturally to a Creatress who has developed her senses so that she can feel her way in the darkness. She listens within and connects with her body's instinctual wisdom, and she has strengthened her trust in her intuitive and psychic knowing. Her journey unfolds as she shape shifts between two worlds and co-creates with Creatress Magic.

Many woman have been killed in the name of being a witch, as something to be feared and eliminated by the zeitgeist of past times. It is now time to go beyond our fear, to re-own the powers of the witch within each of us; to reclaim her gifts of innate wisdom and her natural healing powers and name her a Modern Mystic.

The ways of the Modern Mystic are to find the courage to become the Creatress of her unique Soul Story.

- Re-own her innate creative essence
- Re-member her feminine power
- Move beyond fears and disempowering beliefs
- Re-claim her essential feminine nature
- Go within and listen to her heart
- Sit in silence within her Sacred Space
- Create new empowering beliefs

She has gained new knowledge and now knows:

- Creativity is the core of her essential self
- She is at home in the visible and invisible worlds
- She is a soul on a unique and sacred journey

- She is guided by her passion and her authenticity
- She knows she is Sacred Feminine Essence
- She rekindles the creativity of her Hestia flame

It is through Inner reflection that we create an intimate relationship with our inner wise self. To do so we must be willing to walk our own path; make our own choices; step into our light and have the courage to speak our truth into the world. Your relationship with your inner Creatress awakens your Creatress Magic. To claim her power in our lives we need to commune with the Modern Mystic who lives in our hearts.

Soul Star ~ Inner Child connects us to the Source essence of our Soul. You are a Soul Star, a complex dynamic of energies that together make up the multi dimensional blueprint of your unique soul essence. You are far more than the sum of your achievements and your life experiences. You are a child of the Universe and you have a unique inner light just waiting to brightly shine.

The Creatress and the Modern Mystics together with our Soul Star Essence illuminate a new way of living.

Ancient Archetypes Re-visited

Ancient myths bring colour, imagery and powerful presence into our world. They shape our lives with stories we take into our hearts and give purpose and meaning to our lives. As we move through life and experience each of them we grow and mature over time.

Wise Women of Greek mythology, mature Goddesses of ancient times are calling us to own the power of our Yin intelligence and step into the authenticity of our Feminine soul essence.

They are Hestia, Hecate and Mature Persephone and together they show you how to ~

- Feel into the warmth of your heart
- Connect to your sacred inner flame
- Awaken the presence of your inner wisdom
- Gain the ability to make wise choices
- Hear the guidance of your Yin intelligence

Mature Persephone knows how to find her way as Queen of the Underworld. She has developed empathy and understanding of the Soul's journey and she lives guided by the subtle knowing of her Yin Intelligence. She does not fear the darkness for she knows that darkness is fertile ground for creative inspiration. She is a soul guide and wisdom keeper.

Persephone is the shining one
She listens to her Yin Intelligence and
Decides for herself what feels true for her
Her golden glow shines in the darkness
She owns her Soul Star Magic

Hestia is the Goddess of Sacred Space, the keeper of the sacred flame and her virgin essence is the precious gift of her sacredness. ~ Hestia lives within each of us as we rekindle the flame of our sacred feminine essence. She expresses the true meaning of Virgin as she owns her sacred sexuality and her creative passion. She is the first Goddess to freely choose to be '*Virgin ~ one unto her Self.*' She chooses to live autonomously and she embraces her part in the co-creation of a new world order.

Hecate is the mature Goddess of the Crossroads, She is a guide who assists us in times of transition to make wise choices that are aligned to the heart wisdom of our Soul.

Hecate is a mature wisdom goddess, there to help us step back to gain a new perspective and be able to choose wisely as a modern mystic. Her wisdom comes from her experiences of living, she can guide you to make choices aligned to the calling of your soul. She is the protectress of those in transition between the death of the old self and the rebirth into the new empowered self. Hecate shines a light in the darkness, she is there to assist in times of transitions at major junctions in our lives.

Both Hestia and Persephone found their inner light within the darkness. They are both sensitives who are attuned to subtle knowings and they have both chosen to have time alone and in so doing they have chosen to be virgin ~ one unto themselves. Hestia chose this as her lifestyle and Persephone chose to return to her mother in the upper world for half the year and return to be with her husband Hades in the Underworld for the other half. She made this choice willingly when she knowingly ate seeds of the pomegranate when Hades offered them to her.

The Wisdom Keepers

*As you awaken the intelligence of your inner self,
you become a Wisdom Keeper of Soul*

When a person matures into her feminine wisdom ways, she becomes a Wisdom Keeper and takes on the archetypes of Hecate, Hestia and the mature Persephone. She becomes a mentor and guide for others and she engenders awareness of the Feminine power of a Creatress.

Wisdom Keepers have ventured into the beyond and returned again to lead us home. They know how to ask the right questions and they have developed deep trust in their inner knowing. It is through their experiences of living that they have come to honour the innate authenticity of their Yin Intelligence, they express the aliveness and passion of their Sacred Inner Flame as they live the Creatress Way.

*Wisdom Keepers know the creative power of
Yin Intelligence & Sacred Feminine Essence*

Feminine Empowerment

Archetypes are myths and stories we take into our hearts, they give purpose and meaning to our lives. They are stories that have helped to shape our lives.

Some of us are born with a strong knowing of who we are on a soul level of existence. Many of us forget and lose our way.

You may have been born into a family that did not understand or appreciate your unique soul essence and so it may take longer for you to believe in yourself and reconnect to the true essence of your soul.

> *By connecting to the mystery of your soul,*
> *You are able to make empowering choices,*
> *Create new meaning, and experience*
> *Happiness arising spontaneously within you*

Now is the time to say goodbye to fear and to begin to trust in the quiet messages from your own inner knowing. We all have the ability to make new choices as we enter the space created when we surrender our old stories and consider a world of new possibilities. Are you willing to take the leap into a new beginning as you listen within and hear your heart speak clearly to you?

It is the challenge of this new era, to live a life rich in creative consciousness that honours both light and darkness, so you can enter the sacred temple of your soul.

> *Do you have the courage to reach into your imagination to hear the subtle whisperings of your Soul?*

Archetypes for a New World

This is a challenge for Intuitive Women to live authentically, Soul making and re-shaping a new world.

Ancient Mythic Stories & Archetypes for a new world

>Psyche ~ The Psychic woman
>Persephone ~ The Guide of Souls
>Hestia ~ The Keeper of Sacred Space
>Hecate ~ The Wise Woman

The Creatress ~ the Maker of new ways of living
The Modern Mystic ~ shape shifts between two worlds.
They are- awakening Feminine Archetypes in new ways.

The Sorceress ~ Connection to Source
The Alchemical Goddess ~ Creates Womb Magic
The Warrioress ~ Protectress of Gaia and Humanity

A Sorceress and Alchemical Goddess are connected to Source; a Warrioress is the Protectress for all Humanity.

These Archetypes together with the Creatrix will be explored in my next book.

>Go deep within and ask yourself ~ *"Who am I?"*
>Your soul knows the answer to your question
>A Sacred ~ Heart Centred ~ Soul

CHAPTER 27
NEW STORIES ~ NEW REALITIES

Love is grace unfolding with qualities of courage, beauty, truth and graceful movement that becomes the dance of life.

Stories we tell ourselves hold the power to create new realities.

We are in need of new stories, new visions and new pathways into our heart to awaken our innate wisdom. The courage to create a new story begins with Small Steps that can lead to unfathomable results.

It is a journey that begins with healing your heart and embracing your inner knowing. It happens within you, for only you can know your inner truth that is the origin and the core essence of your aliveness, your creativity and your joy.

Will you join the dance?

The Mock Turtle sings …..
"They are waiting on the shingle - will you
come and join the dance?
Will you, won't you, will you, won't you,
will you join the dance?
Will you, won't you, will you, won't you,
won't you join the dance?"

Alices's Adventures in Wonderland
by Lewis Carroll.

Principles of Creativity and Magic

When we are real and true to our authentic self, we cry tears when our heart breaks open, we grieve our many losses and we need time out to nurture and renew what sometimes feels like a lost connection to our soul.

Awareness is the first step to any real change and empowerment comes from owning the truth of who we are on a soul level of our existence.

Magic happens when you are truely ready and open. Just take a vision, add your belief in it, then add emotion to the mix, activate your imagination and be willing to be open and ready to receive.

Give time and space to dream your vision into form believing it is possible and then let it go. This allows unconscious forces of cosmic intelligence to do the work for you and voilà ~ magic happens!

I have come to expect magic, the kind of magic that comes from living as a Creatress. It is a simple process when you are able to achieve clarity and commit to your vision; your energy signals to the Universe of your readiness to receive that which you desire. The great unconscious goes to work on your behalf while you are sleeping. Often guidance arrives for you the moment you awake the next morning.

The Power of Story

We are story tellers from the beginning of time. This is how we gain a sense of who we are and find our place within a larger picture of our world and the cosmos. When we become conscious of the stories we tell ourselves we also become empowered to choose to create new stories, ones that are in alignment with the intelligence in our hearts and the calling of our soul. This ability to create a unique and authentic soul story is the gift that comes from knowing that creative intelligence is the core essence of the Feminine within us all.

Creatress Intelligence

A Creatress understands the cycles of life and death and she knows a part of her is older than time. She has experienced the forces of nature, the power of creativity and the unfolding cycles of becoming. She has stepped into her authentic Feminine Essence, owned her creativity and claimed her magnetic power.

Ancient Archetypes of Feminine Empowerment

The power to energise a new life story requires brave choices, creativity and the courage to walk new paths. This allows you to re-vision empowering Feminine Archetypes as you connect to your inner Creatress ~ The Artist, the Healer and the Virgin Goddesses Persephone and Hestia.
Wisdom Keepers, mature Persephone, Hecate and Hestia hold the key to unlock the heart vibrations of love for yourself, and to begin to heal those of us who have a wounded heart.

There are many forms of creative magic and many ways in which you can hear the subtle voice of soul calling you to embrace your Feminine Essence.

This is the Art of Creatress Magic.

A Creatress knows how to nurture new life. She takes in the old and creates the future using alchemy and the pure energy of love to transform, renew and reshape each of her creations.

- She speaks to us through art in mediums of image, symbols, words, music, dance and song.
- Her messages resonate in our hearts and can be felt as innate knowing within our body.
- She is found in the aliveness and inspiration of the messages hidden in our dreams

- She comes to us as a feeling or sensation that awakens new perspectives and understanding.
- She arrives as flashes of intuitive knowings.
- She moves through us, just as the river flows across the land and the wind blows through the trees
- She refreshes us and awakens us to our soul
- When we own her soul power, this transforms us and changes who we become.

She is our path to Becoming that comes from the quality of our energy as we honour her magnetic Presence. Others sense this change within us as our energy intensifies and expands out into the world.

Live your Authentic Soul Story and experience spontaneous moments of inner joy

There is something exciting about living from a place of authenticity that is magnetically attractive. It awakens the shining inner glow of your sacred flame.

This path to Becoming is an inside job
~ Step into your power as a Creatress

CHAPTER 28

MAGIC OF THE INNER CHILD

Awaken to the Soul Star you are here to become
And shine your inner light for all to see

Your Soul Star Self is your Inner child who feels free to explore the wonder and magic that surrounds you in every moment. You have come to Earth to learn and grow from all your experiences as a Human Being.

Remember the magic of your inner child
and say to yourself ~

"I believe in Magic"

This Soul Star child within us knows how to laugh and play. It allows us to ponder the wonder and magic of life itself. Learn to be kind and love your inner child, and give yourself permission to enjoy the unfolding journey of Becoming that is your life's adventure.

Re-kindle your connection to the dreams of your inner child. This is how we begin to remember who we are here to become. As we learn to trust in our Soul Star essence, we begin to experience the joy of child like wonder.

Reclaim the magical realms of your Inner Child

Your Inner Child is your Soul Star aliveness that loves to play and explore all the sensations of the world and the wonder and magic that surrounds and delights.

Dreams, pre-cognitions, the imaginal realms and your Inner knowing are messengers of your Soul Star magic. They open the path to your Soul's awakening.

It is that part of us that has not yet learned to mistrust itself nor fear the future. There is an open connection to inner knowing that is pre-cognition, this is the wisdom of the new born child, something many of us have long forgotten.

My inner child feeds my creativity and gives me permission to enjoy the journey of my life. With a willingness to step out into the unknown like the fool in the Tarot with trust in an unknown future, my inner child has an innocence that is spontaneous and very real.

Artistic expression comes like magic from this place of child like wonder. Music, Dance and Song and other artistic mediums are expressions from this creative child self. So claim the freedom to play and experience child like wonder and learn to believe in magic again.

As you develop trust in your imagination and the subtle invisible realms you will find that your Love for yourself grows. Love's energy can be contagious, so beware of emotions arising that are not easily explained ~ you may infect others with feelings of happiness.

*Joy bubbles up from within,
loving feelings wash over me as
I feel a well of happiness arise from within*

*I am in harmony with everything around me,
with a sense of purpose and overwhelming joy*

The paradox is that you are imperfect perfection and your soul has a wisdom that reaches far beyond the perceptions of your rational left brain consciousness.

- Listen into the sounds of your soul's whisperings
- Know your Soul speaks in the language of love
- Your heart connects the innate intelligence in your body and cosmic intelligence that is the beyond
- Your wisdom and power flow to you from the invisible realms of cosmic consciousness
- You are the wisdom keeper of your soul

Bring alive the innocence and wonder of your creative, playful, happy inner child who is curious to discover what's next.

Give up the need to know the outcome, know only the next small step to take as you move beyond your limiting beliefs.

Claim the freedom to leap from one stepping stone to the next without needing to know where you will end up.

Feel into the warmth of your open heart and send that loving energy into your world; feel the awe and wonder of your inner child, that comes from Soul Star living.

When we become aligned to our soul purpose, we experience feelings of happiness arise spontaneously within us.

Signs of being in alignment with your soul purpose

- Spontaneously singing
- Feeling enthusiasm on waking
- Propensity to imagine a positive future
- Joyfulness of being alive
- Openness to the unfolding patterns of life
- Experiences of synchronicities abounding
- Clarity, peace and harmony surround you

Each Soul is surrounded by an aura of authentic light that is the illumined glow of their Soul essence and the unique expression of Cosmic Soul here on earth.

Allow yourself space and time to embrace the truth of who you are here to become.

Your awakened Soul shows itself as a sparkle in your eye and an intensity of light from your aura; illuminating the whole of you with its golden glow.

When we live in alignment with our Soul we find that our lives become simplified and the path before us begins to flow with ease and grace

When you know your self, your heart begins to heal and this connects you to an expanded consciousness of yourself as a Soul Star ~ say *"Yes"* to Your Self.

You are a Soul Star ~ A unique manifestation of Cosmic Source here on Earth

PART VIII
WISDOM FOR A NEW WORLD

Soul's Glow of Eternity Lights the Room …..

ON ANGEL'S WINGS

I breathe the Universe into me
I pause and hear the beat of my heart
And come to a place of stillness within
I breathe out with a gentle flowing grace
Sending my love and caring into the world

I sit within my self and sense my soul
With its gifts of protection and love
I am a soul star in the night sky
A bird that soars and lifts me high
My soul is both ancient and new

I embrace myself as a modern mystic
As I shape shift between two worlds
An angel wraps her wings around me
The wind caresses me and lets me fly
As if I am carried on Angel's wings

I know that source is within me,

Feelings of peace show on my face
My heart is open and I glow with grace
My soul speaks my truth for others to feel
Let me walk the inner path so my soul may heal

CHAPTER 29

SACRED BEAUTY OF SOUL

The quality of your presence is your greatest gift
Colour Your World with the Beauty of Your Soul

The first step to awakening the power of your Soul is to consciously create a sacred space in which to commune with your Feminine Intelligence. This Feminine energy is a mysterious and magnetic force which cannot be fully explained, it can begin to be known through lived experiences.

I began to seek answers by exploring my inner world and I noticed the many ways in which my soul speaks to me, guiding me and awakening my essential soul essence.

Your soul speaks to you through Symbols, Images, and Archetypal characters that all play their part in Soul's messaging. They will lead you gracefully into experiences that are needed to mature and grow into your sacred self.

As you grow into becoming an empathic and intuitive soul, you connect into the invisible realms, the subtle knowings, the great mystery, and the immense creativity and magical powers that are the empowered presence of your Soul.

You discover that you are a multi-dimensional being grounded in a physical form and you are here to experience the unfolding of your Soul.

As you learn to flow with the confidence of a Creatress and step into the grace of your authentic self, your quest becomes to colour the world with the beauty of your soul.

A Creatress intuitively knows that the timeless essence of her soul connects her to innate intelligence and body wisdom and she lives the sacred aliveness of her Soul.

Your soul is here to express the unique beauty of your truth that lives buried deep within you. When you strengthen your connection to the power of the feminine within and learn to live as a Creatress, you begin to know how to create your unique soul story.

Your soul's gifts are so innately part of who you are that often you are unable to appreciate them within you. Often it is only when another recognises these gifts and appreciates their value are you able to begin to see the truth of who you are and the natural talents you have been given.

The freedom to be an open channel for the power and intelligence of your feminine essence is to become a Creatress and your Authenticity becomes your Truth and Beauty made real.

It is time for you to re-member that you are a Soul Star, child of the Universe ~ a manifestation of Source ~ and your Feminine essence is primal Feminine Intelligence, the Yin of who you are and the *raison d'être* of your soul.

A Life of Soul

Our soul is always complete and is always present in us. When we open our heart, we hear the voice of our soul loving us even when we do not love ourselves. Soul is both cosmic and personal, and exists within us and beyond our known dimensions of space and time.

Our Soul existed before we were born and lives on after we die. Our soul knows the truth of who we are here to become which is more than we think we know ourselves to be.
Our heart is the barometer of our soul's wisdom and our soul carries knowledge of the essence of our sacred self. Learn to listen into the whisperings of your soul, it calls you to live your truth on your journey of Becoming.

My passion and my sexual power is the sacred Feminine Essence of my Soul. The world is waking up to the dawning of a new era and Hestia the forgotten Goddess returns reminding us that we are Sacred.
She is our light in the darkness, the passion in our loving heart and the pure essence of the joy within our Soul.

Find the Sacred Space within ~ the aliveness of your Creative Essence ~ La Femme ~ Your Soul Power

CHAPTER 30

WORLD OF A CREATRESS

Live guided by your Yin Intelligence
The Moon and Stars will light your way
in a world of Creatress Magic

The Great Mystery

There is a magnetic force that exists in and all around us, an energy of attraction and repulsion, that is the great mystery.

Your quest is to colour the world with the beauty of your soul and flow with confidence as you become the true essence and grace of your authentic Self.

The mind tries to understand that which is beyond mind. It is our heart that enables us to feel into our Soul's truth.

∼

A Creatress has faced her fears and moves gracefully along the path of heart as she dances her sacred dance.

She has taken the journey inwards to connect into the depths of that which is real and true for her and she has learned how to honour her Feminine Intelligence.

The world that surrounds her is:

> Earth ~ Ocean ~ Sky ~ Cosmos ~ Source

> She has travelled into the beyond and returned
> again to be grounded and fully present in her body
> She has embraced the practical & emotional,
> the imaginal & mystical realms

The Unfolding of a Flower

As the petals of a flower opens to the light showing the beauty of its colours, the inner pistil and stamen and exuding the power of its scent to reveal the magnificence of its essence to the world.

In this way a soul blossoms as it opens to the light to show the exquisite beauty of its colour, its form, its scent, revealing the message of its pure soul essence to others.

When we witness the revelation of the beauty of a soul, this touches something deep within us and opens us to the heart knowing within our own Soul awakening an inner gold that lives buried deep within. This inspires the sense of courage needed to manifest our truth into the world.

Julia Cameron's book *The Vein of Gold* is a wonderful resource for self reflection and the practices of inner journeying in the search to know ourselves as soul.

Energy & Authenticity

We are energy in motion ~ the blossoming of a flower and we are modern mystics who dance between two worlds. As we dance we flow into the energy of each moment. When we are focused and we add the intensity of emotion we make waves upon the ocean of life.

When we come into our stillness we are able to connect into our sacredness. When we are quiet and listen we begin to hear the languages of our soul

Words express the language of mind.
Heart speaks in the language of soul.
Physical body speaks of our innate instinctual knowing.

Authenticity allows us to speak our truth in the way we Live, Love and show up in the world. Our Feminine Essence becomes a shining light, a Soul Star in the evening sky.

Lift up your heart and learn how to fly
Set yourself free and sing your songs of Love

Living in a Cosmic Ocean

Life is like an ocean, and we are just a drop in that ocean. We are at one with the ocean, and we are distinct and unique in our individual drop-ness too. The ocean can be cruel and it can be kind. It may appear still on the surface and it can be powerfully turbulent deep below, with the hidden potential to take on the intensity of a giant tidal wave.

Floating on the ocean. It is only when I relax and lie back with trust that I am supported and buoyed up by the ocean. I discover that the deeper I breathe, the more I fill up with air and the lighter I become in the water. This quality of relaxed breathing affects our energy levels and can change our experience of who we are.

When our energy is aligned to the truth of our soul, we flow freely as we express our pure essence and our uniqueness shines out of us creating an auric light body.

Simple Truths and Universal Wisdom

Life becomes simple, requiring only the courage to take one small step after another, with the excitement of discovery and a willingness to follow subtle calling from soul.

> Trust Yourself ~ Love Yourself ~ Embrace your Feminine power to reclaim your Authentic self

The Great Alchemical Mysteries

There is a magnetic force that exists in and all around us. The intelligence of nature, the energy of Sacred Geometry and the coming together of alchemical mysteries in science and art.

A Creatress is the archetype of the Creative Woman. She is both an Alchemist and a Modern Mystic, and she lives guided by the heart wisdom of her soul. She is comfortable in the visible and invisible worlds, she allows her journey to unfold gracefully and she shines a golden light of her Soul.

Modern Mystics trust in their Yin Intelligence as they experience numinous moments of connection to the pure intelligence and energy of Cosmic Source.

A Creatress is the maker of new life, she understands the transformational creation force of life itself and she holds the power to create new stories.

Sacredness of Soul

"The Feminine and Soul are inextricably entwined."

A Creatress is an Intuitive and an Artist who dances with her Soul. Her feminine essence is strong and powerful.

A Creatress is a Healer of Souls and Protectress of Gaia our Mother Earth and she knows how to honour Sacredness in her everyday life.

The Sacred can be found in nature and in every living thing, and in the numinous moments when we are touched by Love that exists in and all around us. The sacred can be felt when we gaze into the depths and beauty of a night sky. Sacredness is the experience of being touched by the presence of Soul.

There is both simplicity and complexity to be found in sacredness. There is also a beauty and truth that is the aliveness of Soul. This sacredness flows through us when we witness profound moments like the birth of a child.

When we give ourselves the time and space to being open and present to the 'What Is' in each moment, we create an opening to be able to sense the wonder and magic that is the pure essence and sacredness of our soul.

It is in the spaces between that we are able to meet with our personal truth and relax into a spaciousness that reveals the pathway home to our soul.

When we take a moment to be in a quiet reflective space, we are choosing to honour the sacredness of our existence. This dimension where the pure essence of Love exists. We open to an experience of unconditional love and feel into the presence of soul alive within our hearts. Beyond all religions, beyond all cultures, know that your body is the sacred container of your Soul.

The Divine is suggestive of something out there, beyond our reach, up in the heavens, the divine mystery of 'All That Is.'

There is a way of living that honours both Sacred Space and the Sacred exists within us as our personal felt sense of soul. When you give time and space to honour the sacred within you, you open a door that leads you gracefully into the depths of your soul. Everything that exists outside of us in our known world also carries this energy of sacredness.

The Unfolding

You must be willing to stay in the not knowing and enter fully into chaos to allow the creative process to unfold. Follow the energy of the moment and enter into the mystery of discovery with a sense of curiosity, and child like wonder.

There are gifts hidden in this deep place within you which when awoken can become the source of great happiness and fulfilment. This is the gift of your inner gold, your authenticity and your unique soul essence.

The heart has an intelligence that knows what is true for you. It has a power that emanates as a warmth in the centre of your chest, it is a flame in the centre of your being and a glowing light that expands out into your aura.

The heart is the barometer of the soul. It speaks to you in subtle whispers and calls you to live in alignment with your inner truth that is the beauty and grace of your soul. The light of Consciousness expands as we shower our attention onto the energy that is this aliveness within us.

When we become free of our fear of the darkness, mystery, and the power of our creative Feminine Essence, only then can we enter fully into the sacred dance of soul-full living.

Becoming a Creatress creates the freedom to be able to make new choices, become real and true to your soul self and uncover where your passion lies.

Being in the flow with nowhere else to go
Oh what joy to feel your warm heart glow

Your Feminine Soul Speaks to you all of the time. Listen within and connect to your personal and Cosmic Intelligence from Source. You are more powerful in ways that are far beyond your understanding. Soul is always present within you. It is not just a light body, it is the pure essence of you at the core of your being.

When you learn to open your heart and listen inwardly and place your attention onto the subtle guidance that is unique to you. Only then can you know the energy force of your soul and feel its warmth as it emanates from within. Giving attention to your inner flame, it becomes a golden essence and a magnetic force that can be felt as a warmth in your heart and light in your aura, as the truth of your authenticity and the energy of your eternal soul.

It is a magnetic force and the creative magic of love. Once awakened it cannot be taken from you.

When we truly love ourself, then we become real
~ a unique and authentic soul.

Hestia creates her Magic From Sacred Space

Only in my latter years have I discovered how important it is to connect into the sacred flame that is my aliveness at the centre of my being. I have begun to remember the Hestia child who was quiet and happy in her own company. She loved having open ended time to listen into her heart, to imagine and recreate her world anew every day.

Creatress Power

The magnetic energy of creativity is our Feminine power. The more we become conscious of this power within us, the more we are able to live our Creatress Magic the more we come home to our Pure Heart

> Dark Goddesses
> Virgin Goddesses
> Nature Goddesses
> Lost Goddesses
> Alchemical Goddesses
>
> They show us how to follow our inner compass and experience the Creatress Way.

It is through their experiences of life and the honouring of their innate feminine intelligence that they have become wise carriers of the flame of their inner truth. They ask the right question and they trust in their inner knowing.

They have journeyed into the dark mystery realms and returned with wisdom they have gathered from their experiences there. They do not fear the depths of darkness for they know that in the Shadowlands of darkness there lies their hidden treasure that is the hidden gold of their pure Soul essence.

Some of us call it the *over soul*. I think of my soul as infused in every cell of my embodied self. My soul's intelligence vibrates within and all around me. It is the essence of my becoming, the 'I am' of my authentic self and the warmth and aliveness of my loving heart.

There is great strength and power that comes from being able to hear the voice of soul always there to support and guide you.

The greatest lesson of all and the secret to finding your joy is to open your heart to the soul's vibrations of Love.

There are wise women who hold the key to unlock our hearts vibrations, they are able to heal those of us who have a wounded heart. They have learned many lessons and grown into their journey to maturity and have become archetypal carriers of soul wisdom.

> Hecate protects and guides us to make wise
> and empowering choices.
> Hestia connects us into the sacred flame within.
> She brings us home to our Sacred Self.

They know how to set us free from all the wounds that have weighed us down and limited us from living our joy.

They have ventured into the beyond and returned again to lead us home to our pure heart. The secret to true happiness comes from living authentically and creatively in every moment, and knowing that *'You are Love.'*

Connect to your Feminine Essence
Uncover your hidden gifts and Love
The heart vibrations of your Soul

FEMME ~ LE PARFUM ~ FEMININE ESSENCE

*You are Femme, the pure essence
of the sacred feminine is alive within you*

*Find her voice, sing her songs and gracefully
dance to the music in your heart and create
the tapestry of your unique soul story*

I remember my mother saying that a woman is not fully dressed until she has put on her perfume. My favourite perfume that I applied to the pulse points of my wrists and behind my ears before leaving the house was FEMME by Roché of Paris.

FEMME meaning woman in French could also be read as Fem/Me or *Feminine Me* (femininity) which is how the perfume *Femme* made me feel.

∾

This was back in the 60's and 70's when life was slower and there was more time for a private life with many spaces in between; dreams and imagination could be fostered, and there was time to ponder, sleep and dream. This was a deeply healing and restorative gift we all took for granted.

I am now an older silver haired woman but my Essence has not been lost. It has travelled with me and still lights me up with an inner glow. I think of it as my inner flame that is my eternal Creatress power.

I can now stand back and see the tapestry of my life with its woven threads of many colours, each adding a different tone, shaping my experiences as they gracefully dance through the stories of my Becoming.

I know how important it is to keep my inner flame alive. It is home to the fire of my passion that feeds my intuition, my emotional intelligence and my heart wisdom.

I have the greatest gift of all. I know my truth, I have clarity around my intentions, I speak from my authentic self with an open heart and I find my true essence is perceived by others. This becomes a reciprocal vibrational experience, and a transference of the energy of Love. Then you know that you are Love.

Remember too that you are soul, awaken to the immense power within you that is your forever Feminine Essence and own the Yin Intelligence of yourself as Creatress.

FEMININE ESSENCE

La Femme ~ French for 'The Woman"
Pronounced *La Fam*
Meaning: the Feminine Principle revealed
~ The pure Essence of the Feminine
Her truth, her beauty, her passion and her power

Goddess of the Sacred Flame
Based upon the Myth of Hestia, an Ancient Greek
Goddess and the Roman Goddess Vesta.
(The Christian Emperor Theodosius declared the worship
of Vesta to be forbidden in 5th Century AD)

Feminine Essence ~ a power that comes from within
Her Presence aligns with the creative wisdom of Soul

Available to men who do not fear their Feminine Essence
and are willing to risk loving their inner Feminine,
Trusting in the Yin Intelligence of Soul.

ONE LAST THING .....

Thank you for taking the time to read to the end. If you enjoyed this book or found it useful, I'd be very grateful if you could post a short review on Amazon or your preferred Retailer. Your support really does make a difference and I read all the reviews personally.

To leave a review please go to your preferred book supplier or click the link below for the Amazon review page. A review or a Star rating is much appreciated. Thanks for your support!

Review page: https://amzn.to/3IezixF

Review page ~ La Femme Goddess of the Sacred Flame

POEMS

    Sacredness
    Hestia
    An Awakened Creatress
    Love Token
    The Black Virgin
    Womb Magic
    Persephone's Dance
    Child of the Universe
    On Angels Wings

ACKNOWLEDGMENTS

La Femme as the voice of Feminine Essence has been with me every day as my companion and guide, calling me to put words onto paper so that she can claim her presence in a world that is in upheaval.

At this time of being on the brink of great change, where the old life we knew is lost to us and the shape of a new world is yet to emerge fully into reality, the Essence of the Feminine is needed to create balance in a world that appears to have lost its way.

There are those who have chosen to walk the path of a Creatress and live in alignment with the calling of their soul. Their presence has helped me to stay focused on the task of finishing this book and preparing to write the Macro version of this story.

My thanks for the continued friendship and Inspiration of fellow Astrologers with a focus on Soul Essence.

Franchelle Ofsoské-Wyber Spiritual Teacher and Mentor

Monique Leurink Developer of Diamond Astrology ~ A new dimension in the World of the Stars

Murray Beauchamp for his words of encouragement and his ground breaking work and commitment to the Astrology of the Lunar Saros Cycles.

A very special thanks goes to my daughter Marnie Harrison who has travelled many paths from Makeup Artist, to Underwater cinematographer of Dolphins and Whales, and now her focus is on wholistic healing using the power of nature and the unseen realms of the Soul consciousness.

Finally my thanks goes to the writers listed on the *Sources and other Readings page* and many others who have influenced my thinking and helped me over many years to have the courage to connect with my Feminine Essence and the own the gifts of living from my Soul.

ABOUT THE AUTHOR

Madeline K. Adams is an Intuitive Creatress and author who writes of a Philosophy of the Creative Intelligence of Feminine Essence and the Sacredness of Soul Power.

Madeline named the Archetype of the Creatress in her first book. As with most first books it started out as a memoir and then morphed into an exploration of all that is Feminine. This led her to the realisation that the core essence of her Feminine power is creativity and the Archetype of the Creatress came into being. She discovered that living the Creatress way can be full of surprises and creative joy. Madeline's writing focuses exclusively on themes of personal empowerment and redefines the feminine principle alive within each of us.

Her vision is to inspire others to walk the inner path, a journey into the darkness to find their inner gold. She believes our Yin Intelligence holds the key to bringing healing and balance to ourselves, others and our world.

"I began to discover that as I learned to trust in my inner knowing, my ability to become a Creatress grew until I could no longer live by the rules and belief systems that I had learned to follow in my past.

Madeline has a B. Comm degree with post graduate studies in psychology and thirty years experience in

Transpersonal Astrology for the Soul. She writes from her unique perspective capturing simple truths and cosmic wisdom in words that she hopes will resonate in your heart. She redefines ancient Feminine Archetypes and introduces us to new Archetypes emerging in this Aquarian Era.

Author website: www.madelinekadams.com

Macro Feminine website: www.SourceandSoul.com
For Inspiration, Insights, and Inner Wisdom
~ Empowering Feminine Archetypes

Micro Feminine website: www.madelinea.com
~ Creatress Magic & Soul Star Astrology

Join the Soul Star Community
~ For Inspiration, updates, new releases
Bonus offers & other Resources
Visit www.sourceandsoul.com

www.SourceandSoul.com

ALSO BY MADELINE K. ADAMS

The Soul Star Series

Book I ***Odyssey of a Creatress:*** *A Heroine's Journey to Uncover the Essence of her Feminine Soul*

Book II ***The Sacred Dance of Soul:*** *Your Inner Journey to Empowerment*

Book III ***Soul Star Child of the Universe:*** *Soul Poems and Heart Wisdom*

Madeline's Amazon Author page:
https://www.amazon.com/~/e/B079SLMTK8

Enter the link below in your browser

to leave a review or rate this book

https://amzn.to/3IezixF

Review page for La Femme Goddess of the Sacred Flame

Join our Soul Star Community

Pre-release of upcoming Books 2022/3

Bonus offers and other Resources

www.SourceandSoul.com

www.SourceandSoul.com

SOURCES FROM OTHER WRITERS

There have been many authors who have written books that inspired me to begin my writing journey. They are far too many to begin to acknowledge here. Listed below are writers who have influenced me on my Soul's quest:

Helen Luke
Woman Earth and Spirit: The Feminine Symbol and Myth.
The Way of Woman: Awakening the Perennial Feminine.
Marion Woodman
The Pregnant Virgin: A Process of Psychological Transformation.
Jean Shinoda Bolen
Goddesses in Every Woman: A New Psychology of Women.
Julia Cameron
The Artists Way: A Spiritual Path to Higher Creativity.
The Vein of Gold: A Journey to Your Creative Heart.
Demetra George
Asteroid Goddesses

Ground breaking books that bring together Science and the Spiritual realms to offer us new possibilities and new ways of living:

Rupert Sheldrake
Morphic Resonance: The Nature of Formative Causation.
Dr. Joe Dispenza
Breaking the Habit of Being Yourself: How to lose Your Mind and Create a New One.
Bruce Lipton
The Biology of Belief.

Quotes from:

The Velveteen Rabbit
by Margery Williams

Alice's Adventures in Wonderland
by Lewis Carroll

CONNECTION

I value your support and hope to connect with you:

I invite you to join the Soul Star Community
And receive **a Free Bonus surprise**

- Priority notification, release dates for new books. Pre-notice of promotional discounts
- Resources for Modern Mystics, Creatresses, Artists, Wisdom Keepers, and awakened Souls.

Visit this page https://SourceandSoul.com

www.SourceandSoul.com

LA FEMME SPEAKS ~ QUOTES

The quotes in the list below can be used as catalysts for a daily self-reflection practice ~
Take some time to create Sacred Space and enter into your inner world to expand the consciousness of your unique Soul's potential at these times of great change.

Hestia honours the sacredness of all living creatures
She honours the sacredness of the Earth
and the sacredness of her Soul.

She lives in the river of love and flows in tune with the music of her soul.

I began to discover that as I learned to trust in my inner knowing, my ability to become a Creatress grew until I could no longer live by the rules and belief systems that I had learned to follow in my past.

I have awakened my feminine knowing and I have reshaped my world to include my Yin Intelligence always there to guide me.

I have found that the Sacred Feminine is a creative force which by its very nature is magical mystery.

I know the secret to finding my inner happiness is to live creatively and follow the calling of my soul.

I become virgin as I own Hestia's sacred flame.

I commit to nourishing the power of my passion and the sacred aliveness of my inner flame.

I hear my soul speak as I expand my perceptions of the Invisible realms and I connect to the dimensions of Cosmic Intelligence.

I am mystery unfolding out of darkness,
I am the Black Virgin and the Black Madonna
I personify the powers contained within darkness
I believe in the creative forces of my beloved child
My invisibility is a necessary part of
My mystery and my magic.

The ultimate creation source of all humankind is the dark wisdom of the womb that nurtures all new life.

Do you have the courage to reach into your imagination to hear the subtle whisperings of your Soul?

The secret to true happiness comes from living authentically and creatively in every moment.

Feminine Essence is your Creative Power.

Awaken to the Soul Star you are here to become

And shine your inner light for all to see.

*Joy bubbles up from within,
loving feelings wash over me as
I feel a well of happiness arise from within.*

*I am in harmony with everything around me,
With a sense of purpose and overwhelming joy.*

*You are a Soul Star ~ A unique manifestation of
Cosmic Source here on Earth.*

*The quality of your presence is your greatest gift
Colour Your World with the Beauty of Your Soul.*

*Live guided by your Yin Intelligence
The Moon and Stars will light your way
in a world of Creatress Magic.*

*We have a Presence,
who we are at the core of our being
that others can sense without the need for words
We perceive this subtle energy in others too.*

Do you remember a time when you believed that anything was possible; when you were willing to flow from one experience to another without the need to known the outcome?

Sometimes we can feel it even in our bones.

A heart that is closed carries the heavy weight of painful memories. It is full of grief that has settled in the body, weighting you down, sapping your energy and removing experiences of joy from your life.

This is how magic happens as you trust in your inner voice, risk taking with a small step in a new direction and be open to a different story unfolding.

Small steps over time lead to big dreams coming true.

Into the darkness to meet the magnetic forces within …..

Wisdom Keepers are the Goddesses Hestia, Hecate and the mature Persephone who know the power of womb magic.

They are comfortable in the dark realms and sacred spaces where magic happens. They are healers who hold the key to heart vibrations that can heal every wounded heart.

Their innate intelligence makes them wise carriers of the sacred flame of Feminine Essence as a symbol of the creative passion of your inner truth.

They do not fear the darkness for they have ventured into the depths of the shadowlands and returned with wisdom that has been gathered from their experiences there.

There are new Feminine Archetypes making their presence felt in todays world ~

Creatress
Modern Mystic
Mature Persephone
Soul Star ~ Cosmic Child
La Femme ~ Feminine Essence

A Creatress dances between the visible and invisible realms
She values darkness as fertile ground for creative inspiration.

When You Choose to Say Yes to Yourself …..

Many woman have been killed in the name of being a witch, as something to be feared and eliminated by the zeitgeist of past times. It is now time to go beyond our fear, to re-own the powers of the witch within each of us; to reclaim her gifts of innate wisdom and her natural healing powers and name her a Modern Mystic.

*Wisdom Keepers know the creative power of
Yin Intelligence & Sacred Feminine Essence*

You may have been born into a family that did not understand or appreciate your unique soul essence and so it may take longer for you to believe in yourself and reconnect to the true essence of your soul.

*By connecting to the mystery of your soul,
You are able to make empowering choices,
Create new meaning, and experience
Happiness arising spontaneously within you*

Soul's Glow of Eternity Lights the Room .....

There is both simplicity and complexity to be found in sacredness. There is also a beauty and truth that is the aliveness of Soul. This sacredness flows through us when we witness profound moments like the birth of a child.

The magnetic energy of creativity is our Feminine power.

The more we become conscious of this power within us, the more we are able to live our Creatress Magic the more we come home to our Pure Heart

*Dark Goddesses
Virgin Goddesses
Nature Goddesses*

Lost Goddesses
Alchemical Goddesses

They show us how to follow our inner compass and experience the Creatress Way.

Soul is always present within you. It is not just a light body, it is the pure essence of you at the core of your being.

Giving attention to your inner flame, it becomes a golden essence and a magnetic force that can be felt as a warmth in your heart and light in your aura, as the truth of your authenticity and the energy of your eternal soul.

It is a magnetic force and the creative magic of love. Once awakened it cannot be taken from you.

Only in my latter years have I discovered how important it is to connect into the sacred flame that is my aliveness at the centre of my being.

I have begun to remember the Hestia child who was quiet and happy in her own company. She loved having open ended time to listen into her heart, to imagine and recreate her world anew every day.

NOTES

www.ingramcontent.com/pod-product-compliance
Lightning Source LLC
Chambersburg PA
CBHW022055290426
44109CB00014B/1108